Simple Stage Costumes

SIMPLE STAGE COSTUMES
and how to make them

Sheila Jackson

Studio Vista · London
Watson-Guptill Publications · New York

Acknowledgements

My grateful thanks are due to: Malcolm Aird who took many of the photographs in this book; Ernest Hewitt, Michael Baldwin, Caroline Mott, Richard and Sarah Alwyn for posing for them; and Rediffusion Television who has kindly allowed me to reproduce pictures from some of their productions. Lastly I am grateful to Marian Kamlish for help in checking patterns.

Bibliography

Life and Work of the People of England by Dorothy Hartley and Margaret Elliot, *Batsford, London, 1931*
The Costume of the Theatre by Theodore Komisarjevsky, *Geoffrey Bles, London, 1931*
Corsets and Crinolines by Norah Waugh, *Batsford, London, 1954*
Costume in Pictures by Phyllis Cunnington, *Studio Vista, London, and E. P. Dutton, New York, 1964*
Mayhew's Characters edited by Peter Quennell, *Kimber, London, 1951*
A History of Costume by Kohler and Evon Sichart, *Harrap, London, 1951, and Dover, New York, 1963*
Costume through the Ages introduced by James Laver, *Thames and Hudson, London, 1964, and Simon and Schuster, New York, 1964*
Designing and Making Stage Costumes by Motley, *Studio Vista, London, and Watson-Guptill, New York, 1965*
Costume Throughout the Ages by Mary Evans, *J. B. Lippincott, Philadelphia, 1950*
A History of English Costume by Iris Brooke, *Methuen, London, and Hillary House, New York, 2nd Edition, 1968*
Costumes and Styles by Henny Harald Hansen, *E. P. Dutton, New York, 1956*
Early American Dress by Alexander Wyckoff, Edward Warwick, and Henry C. Pitz, *Benjamin Blom, New York, 1965*
Five Centuries of American Costume by Ruth Turner Wilcox, *Charles Scribner's Sons, New York, 1963*
Style in Costume by James Laver, *Oxford University Press, New York, 1949*
The Book of Costume by Millia Davenport 2 vols., *Crown Publishers, New York, 1948*
What People Wore by Douglas Warren Gorsline, *Viking Press, New York, 1952*
World Costumes by Angela Bradshaw, *Macmillan, New York, 1961*
Bibliography of Costume by Hiler and Meyer Hiler, *The H. W. Wilson Co., New York*
Costume Index by Isabel Monro and Dorothy E. Cook, *The H. W. Wilson Co., New York*

© Sheila Jackson 1968
Reprinted 1970
Published in Great Britain by Studio Vista Limited
Blue Star House, Highgate Hill, London N19
and in the USA by Watson-Guptill Publications
165 West 46th Street, New York, New York 10036
Library of Congress Catalog Card Number: 68–24487
Set in 10 pt Plantin 1 pt leaded
Made and printed in Great Britain by
Richard Clay (The Chaucer Press), Ltd, Bungay, Suffolk
UK SBN: 289 27853 8
US ISBN: 0-8230-4840-3

Contents

16916

Introduction

This book has been conceived and planned to help those who become involved in costuming plays on a small budget and with only simple means at their disposal. It shows methods which are easy enough for the talented amateur or the art and craft teacher to employ when they find themselves faced with a theatrical production to design and carry out with the help of colleagues or students and pupils. Some knowledge of basic sewing and simple methods of craft-work is taken for granted; but I have tried here to help those with a little knowledge to use it to better advantage, and to extend it to wider fields. It is possible that in this way productions more approaching professional standards can be achieved, and that the visual quality of the work will be of a higher and more exciting quality.

It is hoped that a study of some of the drawings will lead to fuller research and that the constant concentration on simplicity will guide these researches into an invigorating approach without any inhibiting concentration on detail and realism.

The various chapters touch on most aspects of theatrical design and making and explore some avenues fairly thoroughly. It is not possible to cut off one section of this subject from another and therefore ideas and suggestions put forward in one chapter may well be useful and helpful in tackling problems in some other rather different fields.

One of the fundamental problems facing those designing and working in an amateur capacity is usually the lack of good working space. If it is possible to find a room with a sewing machine, one or two dress stands and good table space—with a sink and some shelves which can be stocked with the basic requirements of a workroom—it is amazing what a difference this will make to the carrying out of good work. It is still better if the sewing operations can be separated from the messier aspects of the work—such as sticking, dyeing and painting and spraying.

Starting work in good time is a habit to be cultivated. The idea of staying up all night in order to get the show on is a nonsensical one—far more mistakes are made by tired workers in the middle of the night and jobs take much longer when people are very weary.

Plenty of time should be given to careful fitting and at the end of each session the mind should be quite clear about the work needing to be done. Hats and shoes should be checked for fit and all the etceteras should be collected together. It is essential that all costumes should be very well pressed on completion. Name-tapes stitched into each garment save a lot of trouble with misappropriation. Hanging tapes are also very necessary; otherwise the costumes have a tendency to slip off the clothes hangers. Care of costumes should be arranged for during the run of a production by the provision of an iron and ironing board, cleaning fluid and washing powder. A constant check should be kept for the need to renew details in costumes and head-dresses and to keep them fresh and attractive. Unless this is done the visual scene may be a very sad one by the end of the run.

It is also important to see that the actors know how to wear their clothes—how to stand in them, how to pick up skirts or handle cloaks. Some people do this very naturally, but some need a lot of encouragement and guidance. Unless this aspect of the work with costumes is carefully handled the result can be disastrous. For however well-designed or made the costumes may be, they will be quite wasted if ill-worn.

Bearing all these points in mind, and working with energy and enthusiasm, all kinds of difficulties may be overcome; and in the end, a satisfying and exciting production will emerge.

Section 1

Greek Drama

Greek plays are relatively easy to dress. They can also be produced fairly inexpensively with the costumes made from old sheets, towelling (terrycloth), old curtains or inexpensive butter muslin. For more sophisticated results, if the money can be afforded, jersey of various kinds is guaranteed to drape beautifully. Artificial silk jersey will give really excellent results for elegant women's dresses, but it is quite possible to get very interesting and rewarding costumes with much cheaper materials, especially if the style being used is one which is going to make use of painted pattern and texture, thus enriching the simpler fabrics. In this instance, it is helpful to use a spray gun here and there to give extra depth and texture to the material; the robes should not be sprayed too thickly or the quality of the drapery will be affected. The spraying should be done after the garment is made up, either on a dress stand or on the wearer; if this is quite impossible, the spraying can be done with the work on a dress hanger, but this leads to edginess and it is much more difficult to obtain a satisfactory result. Greek clothes are extremely simple in shape. Because of this basic simplicity the overall planning needs to be particularly well thought out, in order to avoid monotony. The Greek plays are nearly always dependent on the chorus and this needs to be designed to be looked at as a mass and not as a number of individual people. While keeping to the same basic costume for all actors it is sometimes good to have small differences within the group, either in pattern or in colour; but too much variation soon destroys the grandeur of the massed performance, which when well designed can form an almost architectural background to the drama. It should be borne in mind that it is the chorus that verbally binds the play together and that visually the same result should be achieved. Anything which minimizes the physical differences between the actors in the chorus such as stylized wigs, head-dresses or even masks can be very valuable. The extremely impersonal quality imparted by masks can be most successfully employed in this context. Either full or half masks could be used. If they are made from latex rubber, they will be more comfortable for the actors to wear where so much speaking is involved.

It is within this framework that the principal characters come and go. Their costumes should heighten the emphasis with colour and detail, thus adding their visual impact to the development of the plot. Tone values are most important in this context.

The Greek dress has the minimum of sewing, and as it spreads out flat even when made up, it is especially easy to paint or to stencil. The garments are all cut on a rectangular principle, the main sewing being the joining together of the side seams, which can be done before any necessary dyeing.

The earlier Greek costumes are frequently very extensively patterned, whereas the later ones are usually of plain coloured fabric with a decorated edge. Colours are quite rich, the drawings in fig. 1 show examples of early Greek costumes whilst the drawings in fig. 2 show examples of later dress, all the costumes are drawn from sources in the British Museum.

Only three garments are met with—one is the cloak or chlamys, which is a rectangular piece of material, the length being about twice the width, which can be variously worn. The second is the shirt or chiton, which is worn by either men or women and is found in various lengths and can be either pleated or simple, and the third is the over-dress or peplos which is an upper garment worn only by women. This latter is often folded over at the top, see pages 79–80, styles 40–43, and may be girded either over or under the fold. Rope or cord or braid can be used for girding the costumes, or even ordinary tape will do. It is wiser to use the kind of tape or braid that does not stretch as this tends to become loose in wearing and the folds and drapes go astray, with very untidy results. Girdles or drapes should never be fixed, but tied freshly for each performance. Both chiton and peplos are found in various widths—shoulder width, elbow length or wrist to wrist—and are usually caught at the shoulders with brooches, clasps or ties. When the garment is cut as wide as wrist or elbow width, there are usually several of these fastenings which catch the material over the top of the arm to form a sleeve (see pages 79–80, styles 40–43). Very useful and cheap for simulating these brooches are the old-fashioned bosse like picture hangers which may still be bought for a few pence in old-fashioned hardwear shops; there are also plastic motifs, very often in suitable shapes also procurable from hardware shops, some multiple stores and at 'Do It Yourself' shops. Small holes can easily be drilled in these with a hand drill so that they may be stitched to the costume. They may be painted with oil paint or emulsion paint and then touched with gold here and there to enrich them. It is worth noting that it is nearly always more satisfactory to paint any jewelry or costume accessories with some fairly neutral colour, such as dull olive brown, or yellow ochre and to pick it out here and there with gold paint than to paint the whole article solidly with the gold. This gives infinitely more depth and the result looks far less artificial. As an alternative to these ready-made bosses (raised ornaments) the same kind of brooches can be made in either papier-mâché or in latex rubber. The shape should be modelled in clay or plasticine and a plaster of Paris mould made from it as described in the chapter on mask making. From this mould any number of bosses may be taken. This is very economical when a large number of similar brooches are needed as might well be the case when costuming the chorus. Further ideas for the construction of suitable clasps will be found in the section dealing with jewelry.

FIG I

An effective, crinkly, pleated material can be very easily achieved with wetted butter muslin or very thin cotton. Allowing about three times the normal width requirement of material, the side seams of the garment should be stitched to form a tube. The material must then be thoroughly soaked before starting to pleat it. Two people are required to perform this process; with the material tightly stretched lengthways between them, it must be pulled and folded into narrow pleats of about one inch width. This must be done across the full width of the material. Then it must be tied firmly down the length in a number of places to keep the pleats in place while it is left to dry. It is essential that the material should be absolutely bone dry before the ties are removed. For tying the material tape or strips of material may be used or really wide rubber bands would do. But whatever is used they should hold the pleats firmly together without digging into the fabric too much or a lot of little dents will break across the pleats. When the thongs are untied and the pleats shaken out it will be found that a crinkly clinging garment will result.

Footwear presents little difficulty with Greek costumes. Very many people already possess summer sandals which are quite suitable. For women it should be emphasized that these should be either heel-less or with very low heels, otherwise the wrong stance obtains and this affects the appearance adversely. Where sandals are not available, soles can be cut from stout felt or leather and thongs of leather or stout tapes attached to these and tied through loops across the foot and then criss-crossed up the leg. Some other types of shoes are discussed in the footwear section.

The drawings of costumes in fig. 1 are taken from pottery in the British Museum. They would be very easy to make and there are hundreds more of them which could

FIG 2

be easily reproduced. The first shows a cloak over a simple tunic (*a*); (*b*) is a different kind of cloak over a tunic, both heavily patterned. The design on the cloak could be carried out with a simple stencil. The tunic needs free brush work. In (*e*), a servant girl, she wears an under tunic, an over tunic and a cloak; and finally, (*d*) shows a woman wearing a robe which is bloused over a girdle. There are also examples of border patterns and spot patterns which could be usefully employed.

The examples of later Greek costumes, fig. 2, rely on drapery rather than pattern: (*a*) is a cloak worn very handsomely; next, a tunic bloused above a girdle and girded again above this. A small cloak, clasped at the neck is also worn, (*b*); the third figure (*c*) shows a pleated dress with clasps along the tops of the arms, making the material into a sleeve. A light-weight cloak which forms rather complicated drapery is worn over this. Finally (*d*), a dress with a bloused overfold, girded above and below, and also girded across the breast. The material for this last dress would need to be a very fine jersey. Otherwise, the result may become very clumsy.

Mediaeval mysteries and miracles

Among the most frequently acted plays by amateurs are nativity and miracle plays; these are very often performed in schools, in colleges, in connection with churches, and among amateur groups generally. Their suitability to any age group and the fact that they can accommodate very varied numbers of people, with good opportunities for crowds, makes them very popular. Although they are quite suitable for performance in modern dress, they are more usually dressed in mediaeval costume or in the clothes of the Middle East. There is actually a great similarity between the two. The same simple robes can be used for either; the main differences lying in the head-dresses, decoration and the patterning of the materials. Also, in the biblical countries, striped robes are very commonly found, whereas in mediaeval costumes it is variations of the spot pattern which are more frequently met with.

As the miracle plays were written round about the fourteenth and fifteenth centuries, it is eminently suitable that the actors should be dressed in the clothes of this period. The early missals and psalters are full of charming illustrations of Bible stories depicted with great humour and a wealth of detail. They should be studied closely for inspiration; and respect should be paid to their simplicity of statement. It is worth making drawings from them in order to become familiar with the shapes, also taking careful note of the little details so lovingly recorded. There are very many homely features recorded in these pictures such as pouches, purses, belts, horns, sacks, satchels, baskets, tools and many other domestic details, all of which will add great character if used in a production. There are simple patterns, many of them employing the spot motif in some form or other, which should be noted and used to give variety to the costumes. Head-dresses are extremely important; For the women these are all variations of one theme—the wimple, or coif—which is both beautiful and becoming. The men's head-gear differs among the hood, the bag hat and the chaperon for stylish characters. Most of the characters in the manuscript drawings are of people who could have been met with in a small mediaeval town and its surrounding countryside. They fit conveniently into the scenes depicted in the Bible plays. But there are also pictures of kings richly robed and crowned, and bishops in brocades and furs, as well as angels and devils.

The best materials for mediaeval costumes are those which will drape easily: Bolton sheeting which is a cotton with a twill weave is one of the best, it has the added advantage of taking dye easily. Any soft wool would be good but is more expensive; old sheets and blankets could be used. If the story is turned into a ballet as is sometimes the case, the most successful material to use is a heavy crêpe, for it is light in weight but falls heavily. For men's clothes felt is one of the most useful materials, so is hessian and again Bolton sheeting is very practical. A combination of two or more of these will give a good result. Make good use of rough and heavy textures for peasant characters; sacking and rough towelling are particularly satisfactory.

Use the basic pattern for the robe, which for grander characters can be combined with a sleeveless over-robe or one with hanging sleeves. The robe can be used in various lengths for men, either ground-length, calf-length, or knee-length; the latter may be combined with trousers made from the basic trouser pattern, which can be tied about the calves with thonging. Otherwise, tights should be worn. For mediaeval costume these look better if they are not too well-fitting but rather wrinkled and baggy. Using cotton stockinette (cotton jersey) it is possible to make them fairly simply. Stockinette has a tendency to split at the seams unless it is stitched with a sewing machine which has a zig-zag stitch.

The robe pattern is also used for the women's costumes and as is found in the men's clothes only the richer characters would wear the over robe. Aprons are frequently seen on peasants. Both men and women girded up their skirts when working in the fields or when doing domestic tasks about the house. This can be done in many ways, as is seen in the manuscript drawings. They can be draped up at the side, at the back or at the front—mostly tucked into a belt or girdle. Sometimes the material itself is knotted at the sides. Make good use of this characteristic of mediaeval clothes as it gives tremendous variety to otherwise very simple costumes and can be especially useful when designing crowds; the material should preferably be tucked in, if it seems insecure fix it with a large safety pin after it has been looped over the belt or girdle; never stitch the drapery permanently in place as this usually makes the garment ride badly in wearing, and also looks artificial and contrived.

A passing mention has already been made of the wimple as the universal form of female head-gear. The one exception is the occasional use of the hood by some peasant women. This can be very conveniently employed on some of the characters in crowd scenes, as they can be put on by the players without supervision, whereas the wimple needs careful fixing by an experienced person. This can be a very lengthy process for a designer or wardrobe mistress if there are thirty or forty people to be coped with. A handful of people who have head-dresses which they can manage themselves is a great help.

The main object of the wimple is to hide the hair and to make a pleasing frame for the face. It is usually made of two lengths of material; one is drawn firmly under the chin and fixed with a pin on the top of the head and the other which is laid across the top of the head in such a way as to be able to be drawn tightly across the forehead and then pinned to the first length of material at the temples. The pieces of material can be of different shapes and sizes and can be fixed in a variety of ways. Some of these methods are shown in the diagrams in fig. 3. After some experience, all manner of variations can be evolved. It is also possible to make a wimple of one fairly large length of cloth. Fine woollen material such as nun's veiling is very good to use for this purpose and cotton lawn (fine cotton) is also quite satisfactory. Mull (crash) may be used with good results and is very cheap to buy. Sheets which have become old and thin will make excellent and softly falling wimples. Usually it looks better if the material is just off-white. Under bright stage lighting, pure white can be very glaring and distracting to the eye. To remedy this, the material can be dipped in weak tea or in some very pale sepia dye. The wimple should never be sewn in place or constructed as a fixed head-dress but should be left as straight pieces of material to be remade every time; as well as looking much better this way, they are much more practical from the point of view of washing and ironing. For grander or more sophisticated women, the wimple can be worn over a pair of horns or various other forms.

The illustration shows some types of mediaeval head-dresses. Fig. 3 (*a*) shows the most common form of wimple made from two oblong pieces of material of about the same size. It is easiest to fix this or any of the simple draped wimples if the hair is first combed from the face and the head then bound with an elastic (crêpe) bandage.

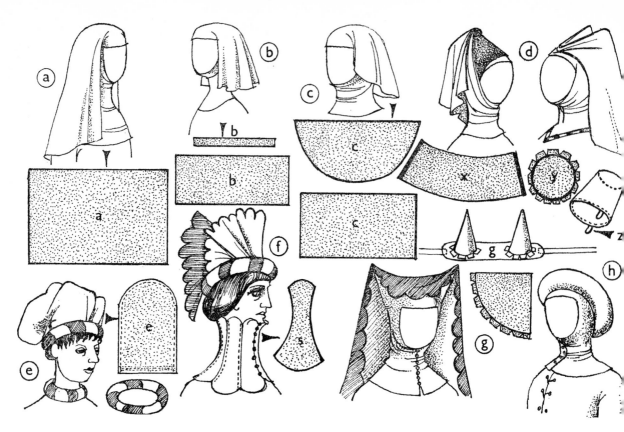

This not only controls the hair but makes a good firm basis on which the wimple may be fixed with straight pins. It will also be found that arranged in this way the wimple is much less likely to slip about on the head. All curls, etc., must be abolished as they will ruin the set of the head-dress. This should be explained to artists in the hope of gaining their co-operation.

Fig. 3 (*b*) is a wimple with a mere strap under the chin. This should be of double material and fixed on the top of the head with a safety pin.

Fig. 3 (*c*) shows a larger drape under the chin and a half circle over the top of the head, with the straight edge drawn tightly across the forehead. A full circle could alternatively be used and a simple circlet placed over it to keep it in position. Two variations of slightly grander wimples are shown in fig. 3 (*d*). These are draped on to a flower-pot-shaped base which can be constructed out of millinery buckram. The side is a segment of a circle as fig. 3 *x*, with a circle, *y*, cut with tabs for the purpose of sticking. First stick the two straight edges of the segment together using a contact adhesive (such as Weldwood). When this is dry, smear the tabs with the same glue and stick in place. The circumference of the circle needs to measure the same length as the shorter edge of the flower-pot. Another way of making this shape is to well grease a plant pot of suitable size and to cover it with papier-mâché, fig 3 *z*. In either case, it is advisable to either stick or stitch millinery wire around the lower edge about half an inch from the rim to keep it firm. If at the same time two loops are made fig. 3 *z*, hair grips can be pushed through them to secure the head-dress to the head. The shape could be covered with linen or even velvet. In the first drawing, a large piece of material (about a yard square) is simply drawn under the chin and fixed with pins to the top of the flower-pot—a soft muslin would be good for this. It should be arranged so that it falls in pleasing folds. In the second drawing the flower-pot is worn over a cambric (very fine linen) hood. Across this, the material is placed and pinned at the sides so that it sits smoothly. Now, taking the material in the centre about twelve inches from the front (forehead) edge, lift the material foreward so that it forms a V, and fix it with a pin at the centre front of the flower-pot and then in such places as it needs to make the shape.

The sketch fig. 3 (e) depicts a man's bag hat. The bag shape should be cut double and stitched at the sides, the bottom edge should be gathered to the head size of the wearer and sewn inside a padded roll. A length of coloured felt can be twisted round the roll before the bag is put in place to give a parti-coloured effect. For the chaperon (f) use a stiff fabric such as felt, or canvas, or sail cloth and cut a length about twice the head circumference and approximately twelve to fifteen inches deep. The edge can be dagged or scalloped and, if a lining of a different colour is used, this will give a very decorative effect. This should be pleated on to the inner side of a padded roll. This drawing also shows a collar which can be very usefully used in conjunction with mediaeval tunics. It is most successful if it is made in either felt or leather; six or seven sections cut to the shape shown s are usually enough. The narrowest part of the pattern needs to add up to the neck size of the wearer with about an inch to spare; first cut a pattern collar in brown paper or in mull and fit it, as the length of neck and the angle of the shoulders must all be taken into consideration. If a non-fray type of fabric is being used the seams should be left on the outside as they make a pleasing feature. Fig. 3 (g) shows the use of horns for a woman's head-dress. These can be made like little cones using millinery buckram and sticking them to a piece of white felt, sewn to the ends of which there are white tapes. These are tied in place on the head and over them is worn a hood shaped to accommodate the horns, and fastening down the front. Draped over this is a half-circular-shaped piece of black jap silk (China silk) with a scalloped edge. The sketch (h), shows a white padded roll worn over a plain hood. These are only a very few of the possible head-dresses but they will form a starting-point for other experiments.

The hood is very frequently met with and although particularly popular among country people it was also sometimes worn by the gentry—it is even seen worn by kings, with the crown fitted over the top. It is sometimes found with only a chin-strap, sometimes with a neck-piece, and sometimes attached to a simple garment. It can be rounded or pointed, or the point can be greatly extended forming what is known as a liripipe. The pattern on page 77 gives details of these variations. Some times the liripipe is worn wrapped round the head like a turban.

Cloaks are important for outdoor wear. In the poorest form they may only be a piece of sacking which some poor shepherd wraps around himself to keep out the bitter cold. The richest versions are made of soft furs for kings and courtiers.

Theatrically cloaks may be used to good effect to emphasize the opulence and dignity of a character and they can either be gracefully draped or left to flow magnificently. Unless there is any specific reason for using a light-weight material cloaks are best made in heavy wools, otherwise they will not fall into heavy folds. Old army blankets will come in very useful and these can sometimes be purchased very cheaply at surplus stores. The amount of material used should not be skimped, for nothing looks worse than a meagre cloak. The cloak should always be allowed to take its own folds; any artificial fixing makes it look very unpleasant. Circular cloaks are very effective and they need have no other opening than a hole large enough to take the wearer's head. When making a circular or semicircular cloak, it is usually more satisfactory to do without a hem, providing the material is not going to fray unduly, as this will help to improve the way the cloak hangs. Painting and spraying can often be used to advantage and this should usually be done after the cloak has been made up. A light spray of gold on a wealthy character's cloak can be most effective and will give great richness when it catches the light. A gold aerosol spray is best used for this purpose.

The drawings in fig. 4 show (a), a simple tunic, first half of the fifteenth century, with an opening at the centre front. Note the way that the fullness is pulled to the front to form pleats. The straw hat and the basket slung over the shoulder are pleasing details.

FIG 4 Left

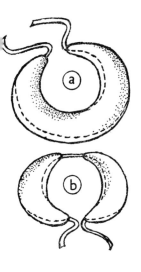

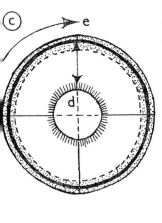

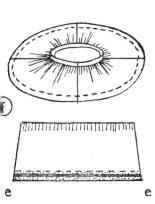

FIG 5

(*b*) From an Italian painting of the annunciation by Lippo Menni. Note the side slit to the circular cloak.

(*c*) Peasant tunic of the fifteenth century rolled down to the waist and with the skirt pulled through the legs and tucked into the belt at the front. A piece of string holds up the odd corner.

(*d*) King Harold from the Bayeux tapestry. He wears a tunic to the ankles, with a calf-length over-tunic. The cloak has a brooch or clasp fastening it at the centre front.

(*e*) A hooded cloak from a wall painting in the Cappella degli Spagnoli in Florence.

(*f*) Fourteenth-century tunic tucked up in front.

(*g*) A monk with a light-coloured robe and a darker hooded tabard, from a painting by Carpaccio in Venice, fifteenth century.

(*h*) From a fourteenth-century manuscript drawing, this shows a woman wearing a sleeveless over-robe on top of her gown.

(*j*) A fourteenth-century fiddler from a manuscript in the Bodleian Library, Oxford. Note the decorative edge to the hood and the parti-coloured tunic, also the belt with pouch.

(*k*) A woman of the fourteenth century wears a gown with either woven or embroidered bands of decoration and an apron.

The various patterns are taken from fourteenth- and fifteenth-century sources.

Shakespeare and the later classics

The very frequent performances of Shakespeare's plays in schools and colleges can be very trying to those departments concerned with the visual side when the production is to be performed in Elizabethan dress. Whereas Greek and mediaeval costumes are uncomplicated in cut and depend greatly on simple drapery, the Elizabethan dress is highly complicated. Some compromise has to be made and so, while bearing in mind that a strict regard for accuracy will be impossible, it is desirable to achieve as near an approximation to the period as possible with regard to the silhouette and to compliment this with well-chosen pattern and detail.

It is with the under garments that the artificial and padded shape of the Elizabethan begins. For the woman's dress there are three alternatives (fig. 5)—a pair of hip pads (*b*), a hip roll (*a*), or a farthingale (*c*). All can be varied in size according to the design and can be made easily adjustable to the waist size of the wearer. The pads or the roll should be cut out of calico and stuffed with foam rubber crumbs or kapok and tied with tapes; both are very easy to make. The farthingale is a little more complicated: a child's hoop—either a wooden one or a plastic one—is equally suitable, provided it is quite rigid. This is held in place by a calico foundation. First make a ground plan of the farthingale as fig. 5 (*c*). The drawing must be made to scale, so it is easiest to do it on squared paper. Draw first the size of the hoop being used and then mark a circle the same as the waist measurement of the wearer in the centre. The length of material required is the same as the circumference of the hoop plus an allowance for turnings (seam allowance). The width will be the length *e–d* plus turnings. Lay out the material on a large table and mark it out as in diagram (*f*), so that there are four gores. Join the seams, leaving a placket opening. Gather the tops of the gores to the waist measurement and stitch to the waistband, use a trouser hook for fastening. Stitch facing at outer edge, put the hoop in position and stitch the inner edge of the facing.

For the man's costume the best way to construct the padding for the breeches is to use a closely fitting pair of swimming trunks as a basis and to build up the padding on these with layers of wadding or thin foam rubber. The trunks must be in their stretched condition in order to do this successfully, so they must either be worn by a person or put on to a dress stand in order that the padding may be carried out

15

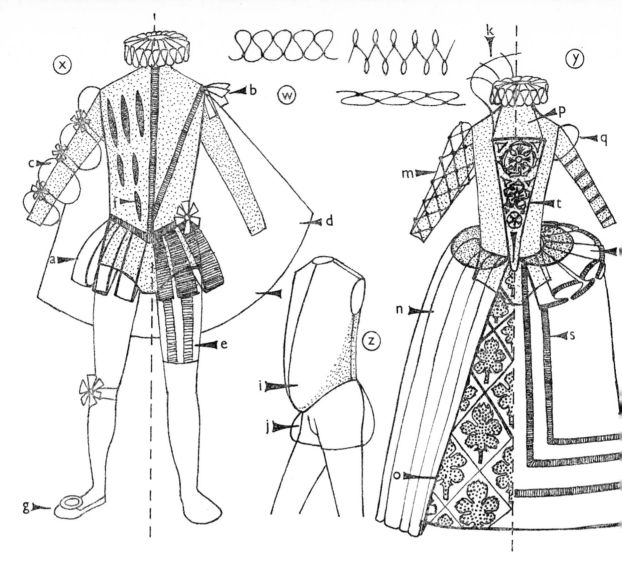

satisfactorily. If the work is to be carried out on a dress stand the crutch seam will have to be opened up. When the shape is satisfactory a layer of stockinette (cotton jersey) can be stretched over it and hand-stitched into place. If this is not a suitable colour for the design it should be either sprayed or painted. The strips of material forming the panes of the breeches should be arranged over this shape.

If the design calls for a peascod doublet it is best to fix this to a leotard. Put the leotard on to a dress stand and pad the front from the side seams foreward. It is best to do this layer by layer; thin sheets of foam rubber are probably the best thing to use as they are very easy to handle and light to wear. They can be stuck together lightly with a contact adhesive such as Bostik or Weldwood, or a latex solution such as Copydex or Sobo. Cover with stockinette as before and then paint or spray according to the design. The paint helps to stiffen the shape, thus giving a nice firm appearance to the doublet.

Padding for a corpulent character such as Falstaff or Sir Toby Belch can be constructed on a leotard in the same way. If carefully done, it can be very effective; it is important to look at the shape from all angles, and to avoid the padding ending too abruptly. Actors with very thin legs can wear two or three pairs of tights which sometimes helps matters a little.

The illustrations in fig. 6 are not designs for Elizabethan costumes but diagrams showing the application of various details to the basic leotard in the case of a woman,

FIG 6

1 Simply contrived Victorian costumes. A modern blouse has old lace trimmings added to it.

2 Men wearing braided slipovers. The masks on sticks are made from papier-mâché.

3 An early mediaeval tunic with magyar sleeves, made in rough woollen cloth.

4 Tybalt, from *Romeo and Juliet*, showing a black cloak stencilled with a white design.

5 Detail of decoration in cut industrial felt and wooden buttons, roughly painted with gold, white, and sepia.

6 Mr Pegotty and Little Emily, using jeans, seamen's sweater, cap and wellington boots, pinafore, long skirt and sunbonnet.

7 Mexican. A brightly coloured blanket worn with a straw hat.

8 Costermongers. Costumes built up from very simple, homely garments.

9 Owl costumes. Felt hoods with attached capes. Felt appliqué and painted decoration.

10 *Commedia dell' Arte* character. Jersey tunic and trousers, skull cap with pheasants feathers, rubber half mask.

11 Bathers. Two all-in-one costumes made from jersey.

12 *A Midsummer Night's Dream*. Design for Bottom as Pyramus. Rough linen tunic and trousers draped with hessian and scrim.

13 *A Midsummer Night's Dream*. Design for Snug.　　14 *A Midsummer Night's Dream*. Design for Starveling.

15 Very simple rustic costumes, including two of the designs reproduced above. Made in rough linen, hessian, and canvas, sprayed and painted.

16 Latex rubber devil's mask attached to felt hood. The beard is of tow.

17 Velvet diamonds appliquéd to a cloak made from a curtain, worn with a lace-trimmed carnival mask.

24

18 Magician. A vigorously painted cloak.

19 Costumes from a play written by children. Hessian and raffia make the dragon. The net witch's cloak has scraps of material tied to it.

20 Scarecrow. A simple fancy dress contrived from old clothes.

21 Clown costume. Vest, check trousers, the bowler hat has tow hair stuck inside it.

25

22 *Laudes Evangelii*. Design for costumes with painted decoration and also with felt appliqué design.

23 *Laudes Evangelii*. Three of the designs translated into practical terms and photographed in action.

24 Three wimples.

25 *Le Médécin Malgré Lui*. Modern shoes adapted and modern shirts with added cuffs and collars.

26 *Le Médécin Malgré Lui*. Note use of plastic doyleys and traycloths to simulate lace.

27 *Romeo and Juliet*. Jewelry made from buckram and braid. A belt of cord and gilded cotton wool throw balls.

28 *A Midsummer Night's Dream*. A canvas belt painted in gold and black. Breast plate with painting and felt appliqué.

29 Rough tweed Norman tunic threaded with leather. Circular woollen cloak.

30 A Byzantine bishop with a hat made of felt and trimmed with braid. Simple stencilled pattern. A collar decorated with felt appliqué and paint.

31 *A Choice of Kings*. Decoration of cut felt and leather. A monk wearing a cowl.

32 *Le Médécin Malgré Lui*. A sweater is used for a bodice with added cuffs and collar. Note the simply pleated ruff of vilene.

33 *Romeo and Juliet*. A hand-painted jerkin. A wimple using two lengths of material.

34 Mediaeval miracle play. Soldiers tunics with felt decoration, simply made helmets of stiffened felt.

35 *Le Médécin Malgré Lui*. Pink silky sweater trimmed with ribbon bows and plastic lace collar and cuffs worn with pink crêpe skirt.

36 *Le Médécin Malgré Lui*. Sweater worn over corset, with added collar. Gathered skirt of cheap blazer cloth.

and the leotard and tights in the case of the man. Fig. 6 (z) shows the padded shape on which the costume is built up. In fig. 6 (x) the basic leotard is indicated by the dotted shading. The panes which are fitted over the trunks shown at fig. 6 a and b are ribbons or shoulder tabs, c sleeve puffs which could be made separately on elastic with only the top puff stitched in place, d is a shoulder cape which could be successfully cut from felt, and e the upper part of the tights can be painted to represent canyons. The Elizabethan jerkin is frequently slashed, this would be quite unpractical with a leotard, but could be represented stylistically by shapes cut out in felt and stuck to the leotard with Copydex fig. 6 f; g shows a bun-toed shoe. The other half of the doublet is trimmed with braid or strips of felt.

Fig. 6 (y), showing the woman's dress is again bisected longitudinally: the leotard and hip pads are shown in the dotted shading, the stomacher, which should be stiffened t has a pattern which can be either painted or appliquéd and should be fixed to the leotard along the top and down the centre. A divided overskirt is shown at n which is worn over the under-skirt o, which has a pattern which could be either stencilled or appliquéd. The other half of the skirt is shown as braided fig. 6 s and has an extra circle of pleated material round the waist which can be very decorative, r.

With this dress is worn either a ruff or a wired gauze or lace collar for which stiff plastic doyleys could be utilized as they are both decorative and cheap. (w) shows three different ways of stitching the pleats of a ruff. These can be made from starched lawn or muslin, but this is not very serviceable and they are much better if they are constructed from nylon crin which is very easily cleaned by merely shaking in water to which a little detergent has been added. Fig. 6 p shows how the partlet may be represented by spraying through boldly patterned lace or a plastic doyley on to the basic leotard.

Two kinds of sleeves are shown, q shows a small puff with the lower part banded either with stripes of braid or paint. The other is a gauze over-sleeve braided in a lattice pattern and caught at the intersections with beads or pearls, m.

FIG 7   (PART I)

Beside Shakespeare and the lesser Elizabethans, there are other classical plays mainly involving costumes from the seventeenth and eighteenth centuries: Congreve and Sheridan come to mind and Gay's eighteenth-century *Beggar's Opera* is always a very popular choice and sometimes the plays of Molière are given in translation. To produce costumes for these economically it is necessary to be ingenious, for like the Elizabethan these are periods of great lavishness in clothes.

In Fig. 7 there are drawings of various characters of the seventeenth and eighteenth centuries designed in very simple terms. This necessitates the use of either felt or canvas or blazer cloth (heavy flannel), or, even better if it can be afforded, suedette. All of these are excellent for the cutting of clean clear shapes which are typical of the men's clothes. The male characters need to be provided with either sweaters fig. 7 *b* or shirts *e* (with unattached collars). The sweaters should either match or make a pleasing colour combination with the sleeveless jackets—if they match they give the idea of the artist wearing a coat rather than a waistcoat. Simple breeches may be made, but jeans, khaki drill or other cotton trousers may be cut off at the knee *c* and *k* and tabs of braid or felt stitched to them to give a period flavour. Circles of felt fixed to a garter below the knee will simulate the cuff of a boot; these are trimmed to look as though a ruffle of lace falls over them *g*. The very best—and also a very cheap way of reproducing lace is to use the *soft* plastic tray cloths, table-cloths and doyleys now available so cheaply. These can be mounted on to a book muslin base with Copydex or Bostik (*f* and *g*). Strips of felt or braid can be stitched or stuck on to the costumes to increase their decorativeness fig. 7 *j*. Suede walking shoes can have the addition of buckles and felt tongues to give the characteristic seventeenth-century feeling *h*.

The women's dresses are based on sweaters; fig. 7 *m* is a long-sleeved woollen cardigan and *p* an acetate knitted sweater. For (*o*) a collar of plastic lace is mounted on stiff muslin. In (*l*) a plain puritan collar is the only decoration, but the over-skirt is draped up over the petticoat to add extra interest. The grand lady has a belt of petersham ribbon with a central rosette, to this are stitched some stiffened tabs.

FIG 7   (PART 2)

34

FIG. 7 (PART 2)

The eighteenth-century costumes may be treated in a similar manner—the difference is in the shapes and the detail. Fig. 7 (r) uses a basic shirt to which extra lace cuffs have been added and a frilled jabot has been fixed to the collarband. The breeches could be jeans which have been cut off and put on to a narrow band below the knee which fastens with a buckle s. The countryman fig. 7 (u) has a hessian waistcoat and a rough shirt t with a simple tie at the neck. Trousers can be tucked into boots. The character (z) wears a travelling cloak and tricorn and the detail of the jabot at the neck gives the costume a certain stylishnessy.

The lady's outfit (v) is based on a gathered skirt worn over hip pads. The bodice w is a tightly fitting sweater to which soft falling net cuffs and a fichu have been added. A small apron is made from the same material. A pleated cummerbund x makes a neat waist and is trimmed with roses.

Victorian Drama

Victorian clothes demand a certain amount of ingenuity if they are to be made on a small budget with simple resources. This is an era of complicated cutting and dress-making and the beginning of tailoring in men's clothes. Unless there is a fully fledged tailoring department anxious to co-operate some easy method must be evolved. A very simple and decorative way of tackling this problem is to give the effect of the jacket of the period by braiding a simple slip-over jerkin so that it gives the feeling of the nineteenth century. The jerkin is best made in woollen jersey and should be made to fit fairly loosely and to slip over the head like a pull-over fig. 8 (pattern as page 76). It can be trimmed either with a silk or a wool Russian braid, which should outline the shape of the coat and then some well-chosen buttons should be stitched in place. The basic material can be plain or patterned; if it is plain it can be painted with checks or stripes, or sprayed to give a shaded effect (see diagrams (b), (c), (d)). Diagram (e) shows tails added to the back of the coat, making an approximation of a frock-coat.

When designing Victorian clothes it is worth getting together some old sepia photographs, an old family album holds a wealth of information. Sometimes old albums can be picked up quite cheaply on junk stalls. For earlier periods see if there are some daguerrotypes available as these give a wonderful insight into the feeling

FIG 8

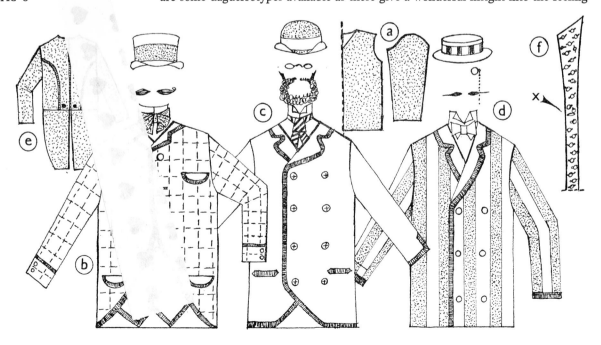

of the period and books on early photography often have useful illustrations such as the photographs of Lewis Carroll and Fox Talbot. It is interesting to plan a production based on sepia photographs; keep the costumes to various shades of brown and then spray the clothes to get the faded and mottled look which gives the photographs their particular charm.

Neckwear is very important. Frequently, second-hand stiff collars can be bought on junk stalls in street markets. Cardboard collars which give a very good effect can be bought, as can celluloid ones. It is also possible to make cardboard collars of the correct size, shape and depth. First, take a pattern from a stiff modern collar and then adapt the shape to the required Victorian one. Then cut the collar out and score along the fold with a blunt dinner knife; experiments will have to be made to discover the right thickness of cardboard to use.

Ties and stocks should always be cut on the cross. Fig. 8 (f) shows the shape of a stock, and x marks the position of the slots through which the ends are drawn before tying. Choose the material for these carefully so that the pattern is in style and scale for the period. A plain material may be used and printed with a potato. This is an excellent way of printing a small pattern on a short length of fabric. It is not advised as a method of fabric printing for large areas as the potato block soon wears out and would need to be replaced rather frequently. Take a good-sized potato and cut it in half with a sharp knife—the cut needs to be clean and level. Then paint the design to be printed on to the potato with a small brush using thick poster colour. The design should be kept extremely simple. Then with a sharp knife, Stanley blade or razor blade cut the background away cleanly, being careful not to under-cut the printing surface of the potato or it will crumble in the printing stage. The printing is most easily carried out if a felt pad is made. This is soaked with either poster paint, designer's colour or ink to which a little cold water paste has been added to give substance and which also prevents too much spread of ink and paint on the material. The paint can alternatively be applied to the printing surface with a brush. The surface should not be overloaded or the printing will be very blotchy. For simple shapes such as spots the end of a pencil may be used or the end of a small tube will print a circle. Looking around, all kinds of objects will come to mind with which to print simple patterns.

An ordinary collarless shirt should be worn with this neckwear.

Trousers can be made to wear with the slip-overs or existing trousers without turn-ups can be utilized and narrowed if necessary. Some of today's trousers already look very Victorian indeed. Jeans and chef's trousers being cotton are very easily dyed. The tiny dog's-tooth check pattern of the latter can be very useful and these also have the advantage of being very reasonably priced. As there is a tendency for them to shrink it is advisable to use a larger size than is normally required.

There are some useful cloaks of different lengths which look excellent when worn over these jackets and trousers. They should be cut in canvas, felt or a stout woollen cloth so that they will hold their shape and not need lining—an old blanket would do admirably for this. No villain of the Victorian melodrama would have been fully dressed without his cloak!

Not only the melodramas but also any plays adapted from the novels of Dickens usually contain a number of down and out characters and for research on this the very best sources are the accounts of the *London Poor* given by George Mayhew and illustrated by contemporary engravings. The curious conglomeration of garments worn by these characters is very picturesque; it will be noticed that the poor very nearly always wear a number of layers of clothes, and the ill-assorted lengths of waistcoats and coats are helpful in creating the right kind of appearance. Hats, mufflers and mittens are all good details. Hand-knitted garments, if they are old enough, are easily adapted to the shabby and threadbare state of the clothing of the very poor. Coarse sand-paper roughens the edges of garments and realistically wears out the edges of collars, lapels and pockets, and a hacksaw blade can be put to good use. For a greasy, oily look rub the garment in the right place with a cake of

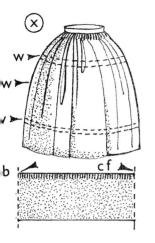

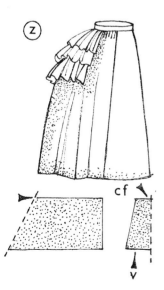

FIG 9

wet soap and then rub a little dry powder colour into it. If patches are put on to the clothes they should not look new but old and faded like the garment itself. Bear in mind that the clothes had usually changed hands many times, would have been worn in all weathers and would almost certainly have slept in. Making clothes look really old and worn is usually a very lengthy process and needs a great deal of patience.

The main character of the Victorian woman's dress lies in the close-fitting bodice and the all-enveloping skirt, be it crinoline or bustle. Fig. 9 (x), (y), (z) show the petticoats to be worn under these skirts. It is worth noting that without a good foundation petticoat no Victorian skirt will ever be totally successful. Once made these form a great asset to any wardrobe. They are very satisfactory if made out of unbleached calico, or from a disused sheet, or old cotton or linen curtains. Fig. 9 (x) shows a simple full petticoat which can be given hoops if necessary. In this case tapes are sewn in place as shown by the dotted lines w and whalebone (which can be bought by the yard) is threaded through the slots and joined in a circle using adhesive tape. Cheaper than whalebone is stout cane which may be used as an alternative, but this is not nearly as resilient and has a tendency to crack. Wire is not satisfactory as it will bend. This petticoat is suitable for wearing under dresses from about 1840 to 1850. Fig. 9 (y) shows a petticoat of the 1860s, when the fullness of the skirt has been pushed to the back. Fig. 9 (z) is a petticoat suitable to be worn with a bustle dress. A quick and strong way to draw up the gathers of a full petticoat or skirt is to machine a strip of Rufflette tape, such as is used on the tops of curtains to the top edge of the material, and then to draw it up to the required waist size. For the bustle petticoat, the front gored panel should be left ungathered v.

Unless the makers are prepared to tackle the intricacies of a tight-fitting well-boned bodice it is probably easiest to get the effect of the Victorian bodice with a blouse. For the production which is on a strictly limited budget existing blouses may be used with the addition of little extra features and sometimes some extra darts and tucks, to provide a neater shape. Again, as in the men's costumes it is only possible to aim at an approximation of the period and a stylized approach.

Where possible, tiny patterns should be chosen as these are by far the most typical materials of the Victorian era; muslins were also popular as these were imported from India in large quantities, as were cashmere shawls. All kinds of trimmings, edgings, laces and tiny buttons were popular. Shawls were of every kind and weight, from the most gossamer of lace to serviceable thick woollen-knitted ones which were used as a protection from the cold outdoors. Elegant ladies wore gloves nearly always to protect tiny hands which never knew work, whilst the poor wore thick mittens in an attempt to keep their hands warm. Little touches such as these, and the use of reticules (tiny cloth handbags, sometimes charmingly embroidered and beaded) should be used whenever possible. There is also the chatelaine, a gadget which kept together all sorts of useful articles such as scissors, keys, buttonhooks, etc., and of course there were fans of all kinds for evening parties and balls, and delightful parasols to protect delicate complexions from the sun. Pretty, too, are the bonnets used by milkmaids as they went about their work. Many of the workers wore garments pertaining to the jobs they did, such as the butcher, the milkman, the pieman, etc., and many of these garments may be employed usefully and decoratively in creating costumes of the period.

Some simply contrived women's costumes are shown in fig. 10.

Fig. 10 (a), (b), (c), show the way that modern blouses can be adapted to give a Victorian quality. (a) shows the blouse trimmed with lace and tiny buttons and the darts from bust to waist help to give the blouse a neater shape. (b) shows the blouse stitched with tiny eighth of an inch tucks and decorated with lace motifs j. (c) shows a further blouse with darts and a lace edging trims the little stand collar and the cuffs. There is a lace jabot n and ribbons on the shoulders h.

Fig. 10 (d) shows an easily made pelerine. The cutting diagram is shown at g. The shape at the back is the dotted area and the front is the dotted area plus the

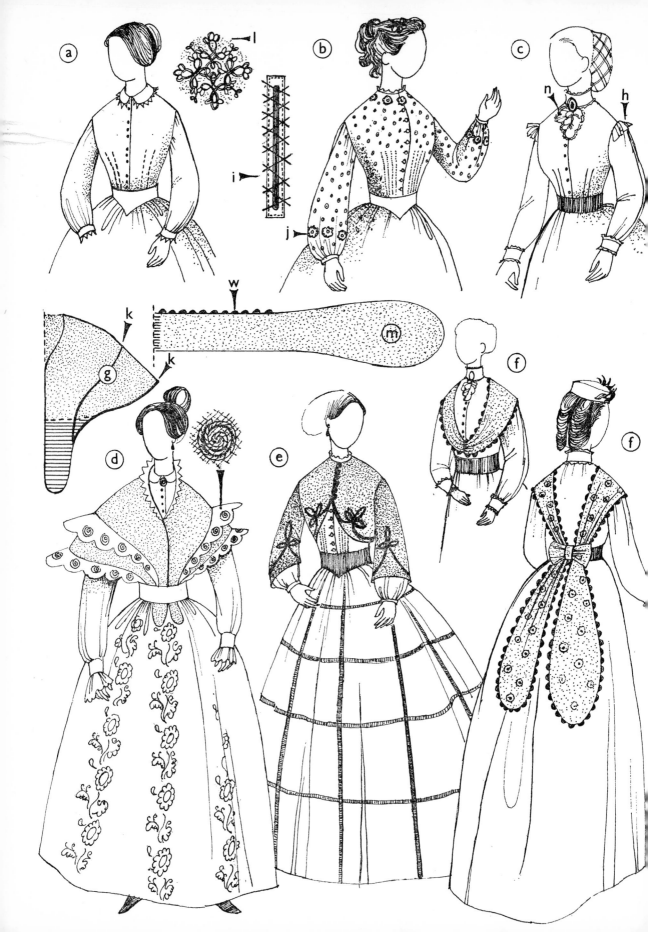

FIG 10

striped area. The flounces are sewn in place on the lines. This could be made of fine net or organdie. Roundels made from braid or piping cord are built up on circles of net and then lightly sprayed with paint, after which they are stuck in place on the flounces. The skirt is of fine cotton with a stencilled and painted pattern. A simple blouse has deep lace cuffs.

Figure 10 (*e*) shows a simple bolero with bell sleeves trimmed with Russian braid. The skirt (of cotton, cheap taffeta or cotton satin) has a painted check on it.

Finally, the use of a soft net scarf is shown in fig. 10 (*f*). It is stitched in place at the front and fixed at the back with a bow. The pattern for this is drawn at (*m*) which shows also the edging of small felt scallops *w*.

There are two detail sketches *i* showing the method of casing a whalebone inside a tape cover, after which it is herringboned into place in the garment and *l* which is a typical lace motif of the Victorian period.

Modern plays

The dressing of modern plays tends to be less spectacular than the designing of period plays but it can be very interesting and when really well done the results are often very rewarding. The achievement of a set of costumes which are really credible is a test of the understanding of character. Of course, there are many modern plays which lend themselves to stylization and specially designed simplicity of statement and these can be dealt with along similar lines to the productions discussed in other parts of this book. This chapter deals with the kind of play demanding a straight-forward approach to realistic costumes which are going to be worn in front of realistic settings. This does not mean that any clothes that the actor brings along with him will do, there still needs to be overall planning and the same principles employed in period plays are important. Regard for colour schemes and the expression of character through colour and shape as well as the careful use of pattern are a very necessary factor. Besides these considerations, texture is very useful and it is visually useful to be able to make use of such different materials as thickly ribbed corduroy, roughly textured tweeds, transparent fabrics, knitted garments, materials which fall softly and those which are stiff and severe. None of these, of course, must be employed as obvious tricks and clever inventions but should be used unobtrusively and should arise from the needs of the character and plot. Comment on the clothes of an actor unless there is a dramatic reason for it invariably means that the character is wrongly or over-dressed. The greatest compliment is for the clothes to pass unnoticed!

Tonal variation between the characters is as important as the differences of colour in the clothes; so is the overall shape of each actor—for the choice of garments can help to make a person look round or angular, squat or drooping. A little judicious padding can sometimes be very helpful—this can suggest a slightly rounded back or a tendency to paunchiness! It is never satisfactory to attempt to make a naturally slender person look very fat—this is because the neck can never be padded and the sudden change from a very obese body to a thin neck is bound to be unconvincing. Any padding used should be fixed to a firm foundation and the clothes must, of course, be fitted over it from the first fitting. Changing the shape of the bust can often help a character. This can often be done by changing the shape of the bra—using a lower one or padding the underneath of the cup to give more cleavage. For a blousy shapeless female losing the cleavage altogether by filling the space between the cups can make the right shape.

Having arranged the basic shape and selected the main wardrobe the choice of detail is very important and extends to the realms of gloves, neckties, jewelry, stockings, spectacles, etc. Hand-bags are very important as they are often necessary for some piece of business. Sometimes these things get overlooked, or left until the last minute. This is unfortunate, as they can make all the difference to the final result and it is not always easy to locate the right articles in the little time left available. A carefully built up character can be completely spoilt by quite a small detail—such as the wrong pair of shoes.

The breaking down of clothes to make them look old and worn is sometimes necessary and this is not always a very easy thing to do; it is so easy for the result to look artificial; it is also usually rather a slow process involving a lot of patience. First it is necessary to give a little thought to the way in which the garment would naturally become worn and dirty and then to set about the breaking down process, systematically working on these areas and not spattering the garment with paint indiscriminately. Sand-paper is invaluable for breaking the cloth and fraying the edges of the garments; a hacksaw blade is also useful. Loose buttons, collars which are coming away and pockets which are beginning to tear at the corners are often helpful touches. The best way to simulate the greasy look of dirty collars and cuffs is to rub these areas with a wetted cake of soap very thoroughly so that it begins to become shiny, if necessary some black powder colour may be rubbed into this. Spraying can be very useful and the parts of garments which get rubbed and sweaty, such as across the shoulder blades and beneath the arms, and where the hands rub the pockets, can all have attention. Very often the spraying is more successful if it is done with more than one tone or colour and these are mingled into one another. Lapels, the fronts of jumpers and blouses, etc., can be spotted and stained as though with food and drink. Red modelling clay is useful for mud stains and mud-caked shoes and boots.

Any uniforms needed will have to be borrowed or hired. It is sometimes difficult to persuade the wearers to put them on in the proper manner, to wear caps and hats at an angle which they do not feel is very becoming, or to wear trousers of a width that they do not think fashionable. This is really important and accounts for some of the preposterous policemen occasionally seen on the amateur stage.

One of the main attributes to be cultivated by the designer who is going to deal successfully with this kind of modern play is a keen and accurate observation of people in all situations and walks of life and to get as much inspiration, fun and style out of them as is humanly possible.

Section 2

Pageants

Pageants are usually conceived on a fairly large scale, often under the auspices of some local or civic authority or at any rate in connection with local groups of some kind. This sometimes means that there is an allocation of funds available for the purpose of mounting the production, though unfortunately this will usually be found to be on the meagre side and much ingenuity will have to be used to stretch it so that all performers can be adequately clothed.

Most pageants have a historical flavour as they usually come about through the celebration of the anniversary of some event of historic importance, or the life or death of some local worthy. Research among archives and books in the public library will probably prove very useful and produce some workable ideas which will give the production an especially local flavour. From the first economy will have to be practised because there are usually a great number of people to dress. Leading characters can be considered individually in the same way as when designing for a play; but the main body of the performers will need to be planned in groups and the massed effect must be always borne in mind.

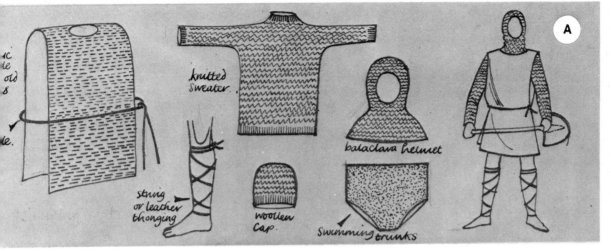

(A) *Mediaeval peasant*

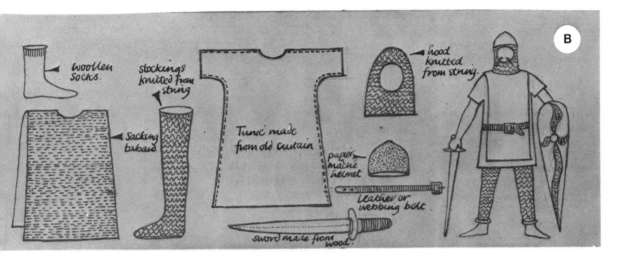

(B) *Early soldier*

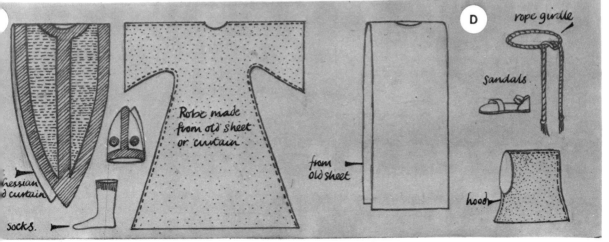

(C) *Bishop*

(D) *Monk*

41

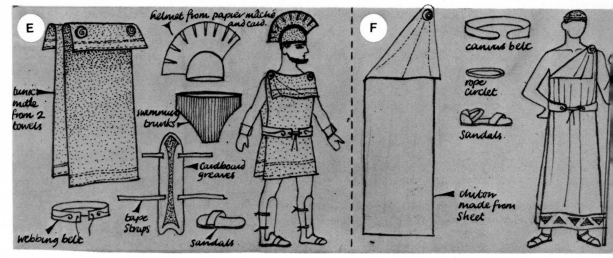

(E) *Roman soldier*

(F) *Roman*

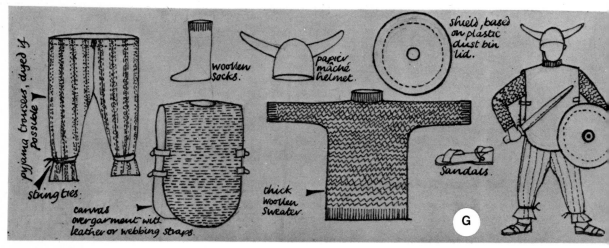

(G) *Viking*

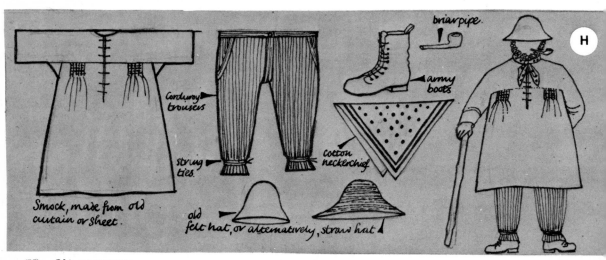

(H) *Old countryman*

woollen sweater

thingade e from 's hoop curtain

(I) *Elizabethan lady*

tights.

(J) *Elizabethan man*

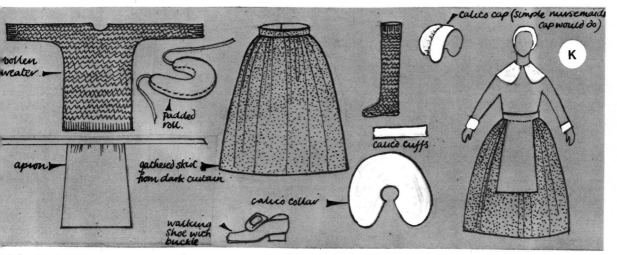

woollen sweater

padded roll.

apron

gathered skirt from dark curtain

calico cap (simple nursemaid's cap would do)

calico cuffs

calico collar

walking shoe with buckle

(K) *Puritan woman*

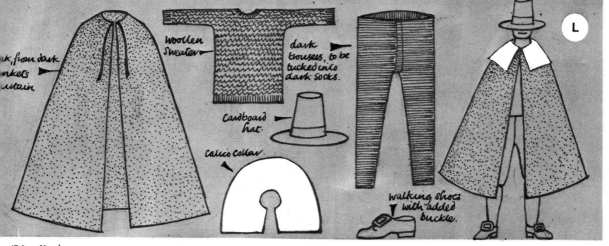

k from dark nkets rtain

woollen sweater

dark trousers, to be tucked into dark socks.

Cardboard hat.

calico collar.

walking shoes with added buckle.

(L) *Puritan man*

(M) *Victorian woman*

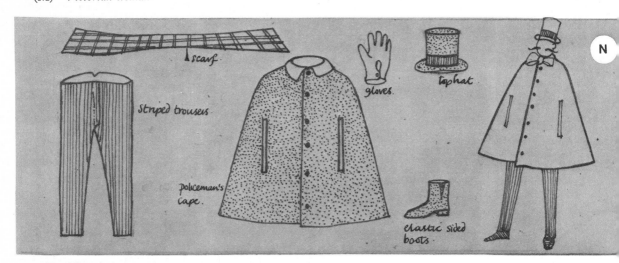

(N) *Victorian man*

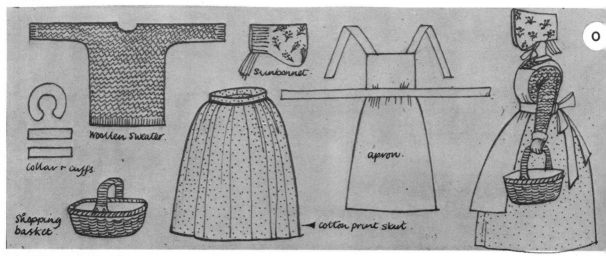

(O) *Farmer's wife*

Most pageants take place in daylight in the open air. This is an entirely different problem from designing costumes which are going to be looked at under artificial lighting; for one thing scenes viewed in the daylight are subject to many more distractions, no longer is everything around cut out by the surrounding darkness, but instead it is very easy to be aware of disturbing movement in the audience or behind the performers. Very theatrically conceived clothes do not always look their best when seen in a daylight setting of trees, verdant lawns and old ivy-covered walls; the same goes for costumes being worn in front of the mellow colours of a stately home. The location needs to be studied and then a decision can be made as to what kinds of colours and textures will harmonize best with the surroundings and conditions and then to carry this out as far as possible on the funds available.

It is very likely that the people taking part will have to help provide part of their own costumes. They will need a lot of guidance in this, particularly as many people who take part in pageants are not regular amateur performers.

It will be found helpful to gather people together in groups and to make each group responsible for some particular section of the pageant. This is often made practical by the fact that different clubs, societies, districts or villages may have undertaken to act various portions of the pageant. In schools and colleges, various classes or study groups may be divided up in a similar way. It is rather like the portioning out of the miracle cycles among the mediaeval guilds!

An opportunity should be made to talk to the assembled company and then to the groups individually, when ideas can be brought forward, plans discussed, and an overall colour scheme decided upon. Reproductions and drawings should be brought forward at this first meeting and, if possible, left with the group so that they can browse over them at leisure and get the feeling of the project. A little later, when the participants have had time to assimilate the scheme but not to lose interest, another meeting should be called when they can bring forward their own ideas and make suggestions. It can now also be decided how to allot the materials available and what can be provided by the performers themselves. The group should now be organized as a working party with a leader and bands of workers for sewing, cutting, painting and property making. A handy man should be co-opted for carpentry jobs which always arise in connection with the props. A wardrobe mistress is needed by each group to be in charge of the costumes as they are completed and to attend to them during the run of the production. If the pageant will not be taking place under cover some arrangement will have to be made for drying out the costumes should they get wet. Either a heated room with rails on which to hang the clothes, or else the co-operation of a local laundry will be needed. If a local art school can be interested they may be made responsible for the painting of the costumes, properties and banners and the construction of hats and head-dresses. If this is not feasible one local art student or art teacher may be found to be put in charge of this aspect of the work in each group.

If money is available to dress the performers without recourse to their own help in the provision of items, it is best to arrange for all the cutting and pinning together of the costumes to be done by one or two experienced people and then to be given out to the groups and individuals for completion. These latter need to be given very full instructions. Otherwise they will have very little idea of what they are about. It is necessary from time to time to check how things are progressing! It is also necessary to restrain individuals from making what they sincerely believe to be improvements to their costumes, for these can wreck the visual effect as originally planned.

When there is very little or no money at all, the garments need to be reduced to the basic necessities. Cloaks and shawls become invaluable, sheets and large bath towels and bath sheets are admirable for draping; blankets, especially bright-coloured ones, can be used with great effect. Skins and rugs and sacks may be utilized for very primitive scenes. Unwanted curtains and bed spreads can be cut up to make tunics and robes and skirts. These are particularly valuable if they are of heavy fabrics, such as velvet or chenille.

FIG II

Colours should be massed together so that there are contrasting groups of dark and light, this will be found to help the visual result substantially. Crowds of people gathered together in a jumble of colours will be found to look quite purposeless and will lack dramatic impact.

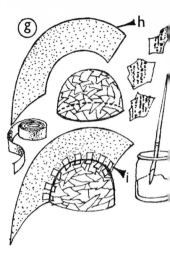

The use of numbers of identical head-dresses, however simply made, are always effective when working with groups. If these are made of cardboard and painted boldly the cost can be almost negligible. Helmets, hats and plumes will all make quite a show even if the costumes are only blankets or sheets cleverly draped. The same can be said of the use of banners, shields and poles with stiff pennants and garlands—anything which will help to have a unifying effect. Any kind of eye-catching device will always go with a flourish and add excitement to the scene.

Some examples are given in the accompanying diagrams. Firstly fig. 11 (a) hobby-horse constructed from a plywood or cardboard cut-out and fixed to a broomstick, and (b) a stiff pennant made in the same way. Fig. 11 (d) and (c) shows two kinds of garlands, one very simply made from a child's hoop and the other a circle of cane suspended from the top of a pole with ribbons and decorated with flowers. The banners (e) and (f) are fixed to poles. The shape (e), if carried by sailors could represent the sails of a ship. As an alternative to the hobby-horse shown here, the more complicated one described on page 47 could be used instead.

Simple helmets which could be easily made in large quantities are shown in the drawings fig. 12 (g) to (j). The skull shape should be made from papier-mâché, using a mould for quantities, and the cardboard shape h added later. This is first held in place by pieces of brown paper gum strip and then secured with the addition of further papier-mâché layers. An alternative is to use the same basic shape, add a cardboard visor and a plume of crêpe paper feathers (j). The feathers should be threaded through a cardboard tube which has been previously fixed to the helmet and the wires should go through the top of the helmet and be stitched in place on the inside (k). (l) shows a very simple tabard and (m) a cloak, either of which could be decorated with appliqué or paint very quickly and produced in large quantities.

Some pictorial examples are given on pages 41–44 for the building up of costumes in the simplest way possible and these may in turn suggest further ideas for the creation of particular characters and scenes. Once the mind begins to work in this simple way some quite amusing solutions are found to what at first seemed quite insoluble problems.

(A) *Mediaeval peasant* Knitted sweater, swimming trunks, balaclava helmet or woollen cap, tunic made from old sacks with rope girdle, string or leather thonging for legs.

(B) *Early soldier* Tunic made from old curtain, sacking tabard, knitted string stockings with woollen socks, knitted string hood, papier-mâché helmet, leather belt, sword and shield.

(C) *Bishop* Robe made from old sheet or curtain, painted hessian (burlap), painted cardboard mitre, socks—worn over plimsolls (sneakers).

(D) *Monk* Robe similar to bishop's robe, over-robe from old sheet, rope girdle, sandals, hood.

(E) *Roman soldier* Bath towels forming tunic, swimming trunks, webbing belt, greaves made from cardboard, helmet from papier-mâché and cardboard, toeless sandals.

(F) *Roman* Chiton made from sheet, webbing belt, rope circlet for head, toeless sandals.

(G) *Viking* Pyjama trousers with string ties, thick woollen sweater, canvas over-tunic with leather straps, woollen socks, sandals, papier-mâché helmet, shield, sword.

(H) *Old countryman* Smock made from old curtain or sheet, corduroy trousers with string ties, felt or straw hat, neckerchief, boots.

(I) *Elizabethan lady* Woollen sweater, farthingale made from child's hoop, skirt from an old curtain with painted decoration, ruff.

FIG 12

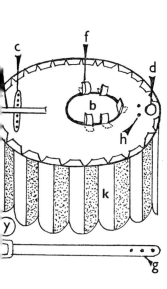

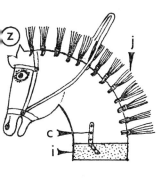

(J) *Elizabethan man* Sweater, tights, sleeveless coat made from canvas or stiff fabric, ruff, garters with rosettes, shoes with rosettes.

(K) *Puritan woman* Woollen sweater, skirt worn over padded roll, apron, stockings, walking shoes with buckles added, dark stockings, collar, cuffs, cap.

(L) *Puritan man* Woollen sweater, dark trousers worn inside socks, walking shoes worn with buckles. Cloak made from dark blanket or curtain, calico collar, cardboard hat.

(M) *Victorian woman* Full gathered skirt, cotton print blouse, woollen shawl, gloves, bonnet.

(N) *Victorian man* Striped trousers, scarf, cape or cloak, gloves, top hat, elastic-sided boots.

(O) *Farmer's wife* Sweater, cotton print skirt, apron, sunbonnet, shopping basket, collar and cuffs.

Hobby-horses provide an excellent way of presenting riders on horseback or an army riding into battle—or knights jousting. These can be produced very easily with the help of a competent carpenter. Two shapes are cut from plywood for the horse's head fig. 13 (z) and the body (y). The oval body shape has a slot a to take the head, which is slipped into the slot and fixed with brackets c. The dotted part of the head i is below the body. The oval hole b is for the wearer's body and needs to be big enough to go over the head and shoulders and when over this part of the body the wearer turns round to face front. Tape slots f are glued round this hole to take the belt g, which is fastened securely round the waist. A hole is made d to take the tail—this is of raffia glued inside a cardboard tube. Two holes are drilled h and a small bag of sand tied through these to offset the weight of the head and keep the horse in a level position. Material—deckchair canvas is very good—is glued on to the body k and may also cover the top as well. For the construction of the mane, holes are drilled at intervals into the neck and bundles of raffia threaded through and then bound and tied. Fig. 13 (x) shows the completed hobby-horse in action.

Pantomimes

Pantomimes, like pageants, need to be very well planned, and it is essential that initial organization should begin many weeks in advance of the production date. Pantomimes are nearly always divided into separate scenes, very often taking place in different countries or even in different centuries. It is therefore very necessary that there should be an overall unity of design culminating in the grand finale. This latter is really just an excuse for visual effects, and for once the performers become merely clothes hangers on which to put elaborate garments.

The scenes should be discussed at some length with the producer so that the background which is decided upon does not present impossibilities for the provision of costumes within the budget or insuperable making problems for the wardrobe. Because of the large numbers of costumes needed full use must be made of the cheapest materials available, such as tarlatan (thin, stiff, open-weave muslin) nets and inexpensive cottons and taffetas. Very often it is possible to pick up goods that have been substantially reduced in price as cheap lines either in the big stores or on stalls in street markets.

Costumes for pantomimes need to be imaginative, gay and fairly bold in conception—this does not mean that they need to be garish. Usually in one scene there needs to be the flavour of what is newest at the moment in clothes. It is always a good idea to make use of a modern gimmick and to point it in some way if this can be conveniently fitted into the scheme. The audience comes to the pantomime to have the eye feasted as much as for any other purpose, thus making a great chance for the designer to excel. Because of the very varied audience to be catered for there must be costumes to please patrons of all ages and delight the eyes of toddlers, teenagers, parents and grandparents.

FIG 13

Usually there is the chance for some country scene involving merry-making peasants in ginghams, stripes or chintzes. There may be a military or naval routine or some number emphasizing precision and calling for trim slick costumes. There is certain to be a ballet which is to look fairy-like or romantic and pretty and which may well need either classical or romantic tutus. The finale, which must be the most spectacular of all, is often set in a ballroom or palace where all the characters come together to make their final bows; and it is for this scene that the glitter of sequins and jewels, the sparkle of tinsel, the gold and silver materials and the waving plumes should be saved.

It may be helpful to examine the different characters and the various scenes in which they are likely to appear. They remain much the same in all pantomimes; the flavour varying according to the setting—so that a dash of the Orient, or the particular feeling of a historical epoch is added to the standard costume.

THE DEMON KING This character is a survival from the days of the Victorian pantomime and has all the elements of the villain of the melodrama. He has usually a leotard and tights upon which there is a certain amount of decoration and glitter—an excuse for some appliqué of metallic and shiny materials which will catch the spotlight in which he very often appears on the darkened stage. He is certain to need a voluminous cloak in which to conceal himself, which might well be dark on the outside and spangled within so that when he throws it back there is a sudden flash of brightness. This character will need a fairly elaborate head-dress which could incorporate a half mask. The face will need some eery make-up and the hands will also need some attention.

THE FAIRY QUEEN This character, representing goodness and light and always at hand to wave her wand when things are looking very grim indeed, wears a costume based on the romantic tutu of the Victorian era. This is a tight-fitting bodice with a skirt made up of many layers of net or tulle. The skirt is usually calf-length, for if it is too long it can look very frumpish and unbecoming. To make a pleasing shape when the wearer spins around it is better if the layers of the skirt are cut from a circle and gathered rather than from straight lengths of material. The skirt layers should be stitched on to a basque at about one-inch intervals and then the hem-length adjusted accordingly. Wings are often needed or a cloak of some gauzy material may be used, which, if attached to the wrists, will look like butterfly's wings when the arms are raised. To complete the costume a delicate crown, with pendant jewels which twinkle in movement and a fairy wand must be designed; the stick of the wand should be long enough to touch the ground to avoid any kind of flag waving effect.

THE DAME The most important character is undoubtedly the dame, whether she is Mother Goose, Widow Twankey, the two Ugly Sisters or some other nursery rhyme personage. Nearly always she is played by a male comedian, who whilst fitting in with the great tradition of pantomime dames needs also to express his own personality. This means that the costumes must be planned to fit closely with his individual style as well as suiting the situations with which he is involved. He needs to have many changes of costume and although these need to be bizarre they should never be cluttered or the wit will be lost in a welter of useless detail. Unless his métier is that of a female impersonator, the clothes should be so designed that the audience is fully aware that here is a man dressed up as a woman and not a person in disguise. Amusing clothes must be supplied for all the old well-tried jokes: corsets, numerous petticoats and pantalettes (bloomers) are all good fun and should be respected as part of tradition. Much can be made of lace caps, bonnets and preposterous hats, and there is usually a chance to design a costume which pokes fun at the latest fashions. Elastic-sided boots are the traditional footwear for dames—worn with striped cotton stockings—and these can be worn from the beginning of the pantomime to the end.

PRINCIPAL BOY Very well-fitting tights are essential and high-heeled court shoes or boots which give the illusion of an even longer leg. With these are worn a variety of tunics, which are always very brief and cut to reveal the figure; sometimes these are in the shape of a gilet (waistcoat), when a long-sleeved shirt is worn underneath. A jaunty hat can be an asset. For the finale, a flowing cloak looks very handsome and the tunic can be elaborately embroidered or painted and spattered with sequins to give extra glamour.

PRINCIPAL GIRL Usually the principal girl wears a number of pretty dresses made with a neat well-fitting bodice. The skirts need to be full enough to be easy to dance in and to look attractive in movement. Ginghams and crisp cottons are usually very satisfactory and muslin can look charming. Rows of braid and knots of ribbon could well be used for trimming. Many useful ideas may be obtained by looking at some pictures of peasant costumes. By the time the finale is reached the girl who started off as a simple country maiden has usually become a princess and must be dressed accordingly. Silks and satins replace simpler materials with trimmings of tinsel and sequins. A plain satin court shoe with a lower heel than that worn by the principal boy is suitable for wearing throughout. With regards to head-dress, ribbons and flowers in the hair are usually sufficient, whilst the finale calls for a jewelled tiara.

BROKER'S MEN These are the characters who are going to supply the slapstick and the knock-about comedy. One is usually the leader and the other the stooge and their costumes need to be designed accordingly. The proportions of the garments may be exaggerated—trousers may be far too long and baggy, or they may be short and shrunken-looking. Whatever style is decided upon it is usually necessary for the wearer to be able to move very easily and to perform all kinds of antics. If there is to be a scene in which the characters become covered in water or flour it is essential that the clothes should be very easily washable and of a quick-drying fabric which can be dried out between performances. Plimsolls (sneakers) are the most satisfactory kind of shoes or canvas ankle boots with rubber soles. Cloth caps, bowler hats or old top hats form a good basis for the kind of headgear which is most usually worn.

POP GROUPS, CONJURORS, JUGGLERS, ACROBATS, ILLUSIONISTS, ETC. Usually in these categories the performers have their own costumes which are especially suited to the work which they have to do. If possible it is advisable to try to blend these costumes into the general scheme without in any way upsetting the performances; this may sometimes be done by altering colour schemes without changing the form of the garment or by the style of trimmings.

JUVENILES There is usually a team of young children who perform various numbers, often involving dancing and some simple acrobatic work. Garments which are elaborate look overpowering on small bodies, therefore it is advisable when designing for children to keep the costumes very simple. The proportion of the designs must be considered carefully, as the child's figure needs quite a different approach from that of the adult. The inexperienced young performer should find the costume easy to wear and he should not be saddled with heavy head-dresses, or skirts and cloaks which are difficult to manage. Masks must be easy to see through. It is advisable that the juveniles should rehearse with their costumes, masks and head-gear well in advance of the performance so that they are quite familiar with them before the excitement of the first night.

The children frequently take part in a school scene, dressed primly in old-fashioned uniforms, or in woodland settings as elves and fairies and rabbits. Animals, birds and butterflies are always popular and all of these costumes can be based on leotards and simple drapes and head-dresses. Sometimes there is a toy ballet and the children may wear the basic all-over garment and masks as teddy bears (see page 20); or dress in pyjama trousers, shirts and felt waistcoats as golliwogs, wearing masks made from old black stockings and wigs of dyed cotton mop heads; or they may be wax dolls or puppets or tumbling clowns. At all events the shapes should be kept very simple with design applied either by means of appliqué or painting. Wings and tails are always a problem and it is essential that they should be kept

FIG 14

small and very light in weight and fixed to the body with some kind of braces so that they remain rigid. If they are merely stitched to the costume they will drag away and droop pitifully. Guidance on wings and tail construction will be found in another chapter.

CHORUS The backbone of every pantomime is the chorus; a band of girls who usually both dance and sing, at the same time showing a shapely leg. They appear in a variety of scenes and situations and consequently have a large number of costume changes. These need to be planned in such a way that they look varied without involving too much making and expense. The best way to do this is usually to base all the costumes on one basic garment such as a sleeveless leotard worn with silk tights or a two-piece bathing suit. This will work out very much cheaper than supplying a number of entirely different costumes and it will facilitate the girls' changes. Head-dresses are fairly important and can make the outfits look very stylish. Most important in designing for the chorus is the consideration of massed effect—single costumes are of no moment, it is the massed effect of identical costumes which counts.

Identical court shoes may be worn throughout, white satin ones may easily be dyed the right colour with Dylon dye diluted with methylated spirit and applied with a wad of cotton wool. Lengths of skirts, etc., need to be checked when the girls are lined up, otherwise the individuals look ragged when they come together as a troupe. In fig. 14 there are some suggestions for chorus costumes with minimal changes. In all cases the tights are the same—a dark blue being a convenient colour for all the outfits.

(*a*) Shows a pirate with hat, earrings, striped sweater, and black knee-length socks (*b*) worn over the tights and matching the court shoes.

(*c*) A drummer with a shako (a high military dress hat) which has a small feather duster for a plume. A red long-sleeved sweater is worn with épaulettes which popper (snap) into place. White gauntlets (long gloves with flaring cuffs) of stiffened felt *d* and garters with tassels complete the costume *e*.

(*f*) A sailor. A sleeveless leotard with a pleated skirt *h* worn over it and a sailor's collar made from felt *g*. Striped blue and white knee-length socks would look amusing, *i*.

(*j*) A soldier. The same red sweater as for (*c*), but without the épaulettes and with a white belt and sash instead *l*, white felt gauntlet gloves *k* and a bearskin *m*. This latter can be made by sticking a great number of curls of black crêpe paper all over a felt or papier-mâché shape.

The second row shows costumes based on a bikini.

(*n*) A Hula Hula girl with a garland of tissue paper flowers on her head *p* and a bra with flowers *q*. The skirt is made of knotted hanks of raffia threaded on to a broad elastic and poppered on to the pants.

(*r*) A finale costume. A transparent sleeveless cloak with a sparkling choker necklace, long gloves and a spectacular hat *t*.

(*u*) A moth or butterfly with a harlequin flavour. A circular piece of chiffon or organza with appliquéd spots *w* is worn over a bikini; a mask *v* and a head-dress with pendant jewels.

(*x*) An Eastern slave. Jewels and strings of beads are draped from the bra *z* and a draped loin-cloth is worn over the pants. The head-dress *y* is a large turban built up on a stiffened net foundation.

MALE CHORUS Sometimes there is a group of young male singers and dancers. If they are fitted with identical well-fitting trousers and shoes they may then effect changes by wearing shirts of different colours and styles and a variety of waistcoats and slip-over tunics.

Animals are included in many stories: Dick Whittington's Cat, the Goose that lays the Golden Eggs and the amusing and popular Two-Man Horse. These must be considered in relation to the way the character is being envisaged. The chapter on animal costumes discusses some of the problems.

FIG 15 Left

Mention should also be made of trick costumes, which are sometimes employed and details of two are given here fig. 15. These are comic characters: (*a*) shows the construction of a figure which can be either man height or much taller. It is virtually a tent on a pole which is controlled by the artist underneath. The head could be based on a vinyl ball which is fixed to a pole *f*. The tent shape is gathered in at the neck and has canes or whalebone let into it at intervals so that it maintains its shape *e*. Net panels *g* must be inserted so that the actor can see where he is going when he is holding the figure at different heights. The arms are stuffed with foam rubber and will have a movement of their own as the dummy is moved about.

The second figure (*b*) stays constantly at the same height—this construction could also be used for giants and ogres. A deep webbing belt grips the waist tightly and has braces stitched to it fig. 15 *h*. The pole fits into two slots of webbing *i*. The hands of the figure are attached to sticks *d* and thus the actions of the arms can be controlled. Avoid making the construction heavy by overloading the figure with weighty decoration.

This covers most of the important characters met with in pantomimes, but others may be included and must then be designed within the existing framework.

Dragons being very frequent inhabitants of the pantomime world a diagram for the construction of a very simple one is given in fig. 16 (*a*). It comprises three parts—a coat, trousers (*b*) and a head-dress *f*. These should be made in something stiff like hessian (burlap) or canvas which is easy to paint. The trousers are made like pyjamas and a fringe of raffia is stitched around the legs. The jacket can be like a pyjama jacket with a centre back seam which is shaped and extended to form the back and tail. Along this a stout cane is stitched. Before joining up the back seam insert a length of tape to which raffia has been machine stitched *c*. Join (sew) up the coat. Tie the raffia into bundles to form spikes *m* sew raffia ties to the front opening and a fringe of raffia around the sleeves *l*. In order to keep the back of the dragon rigid, follow fig. 16 (*e*). Cut a length of cane (bamboo) *i* and join the two ends together with tape *j*; attach further tapes *k* to the two ends of the cane. The tape *j* goes behind the back and the tapes *k* are tied at the centre front. Fig. 16 (*b*) shows how this works on the body with the two cane supports stitched together at *g*. A papier-mâché head is made and glued to a hood of the same material as the body, the raffia spikes being continued up the back of the hood. The whole costume can then be assembled and painted so that it fits suitably with the rest of the pantomime.

FIG 16

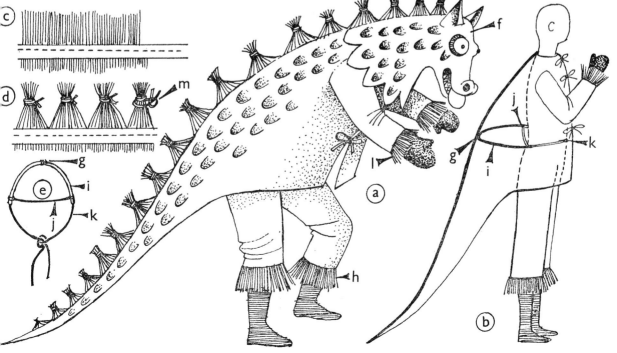

Animal and bird costumes

It is usually in connection with children's plays and ballets that animal and bird costumes are called for and these can be both difficult and expensive to make. It is better not to aim at realism but to try and capture the spirit or character of the animal in the simplest way possible, very often using a bathing costume or leotard and tights as a basis and adding suitable accessories. A mask or head-dress is a necessity, and its style should be decided by the kind of action in which the actor is involved. If the character is going to speak a great deal, then it is usually better to avoid a full mask, and to evolve a half mask so that the mouth is quite free and therefore the speech is unmuffled.

Imaginative use should be made of materials which will suggest the appearance and texture of hair, fur and feathers. Plumber's tow (or raffia) which is easily dyed is very cheap and can be used with great effect to create lions' manes or horses' tails. Bristles from brushes will make stiff short manes and can also be used for whiskers. String ordinarily used for knitting dishcloths, raffia and rug wool can all be used in conjunction with papier-mâché and felt. It is important when using these materials that the basic form should not be lost in an excess of woolly shapelessness. Tissue, crêpe and other kinds of paper can be used very decoratively, and may be cut into fringed tufts, scales and feather shapes which can be stuck on to a papier-mâché base in overlapping layers. Paper can be drawn against the back of a knife in such a way that it will curl very nicely, and if this is done before the pieces are stuck in place an excellent effect will be achieved. Small pieces of net, organdie or book muslin (very stiff muslin) may be used in this way, but instead of curling these against a knife they should be pulled into shape and then given a slight spray of shellac so that they hold their shape. Tufts of net can effectively be stitched or stuck to leotards to give a feathery texture, being careful always to build up a definite shape.

If the neat shape of a leotard and tights is not really suitable, very often a loosely cut all over garment will be acceptable. This may be adjusted in shape so that it can be worn over a padding constructed of foam rubber, see fig. 17 (b) and (c); (d) shows a section of the padding, with the dotted line representing a piece of stockinette

FIG 17

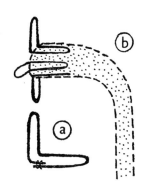

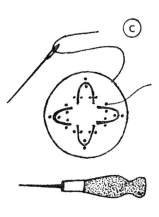

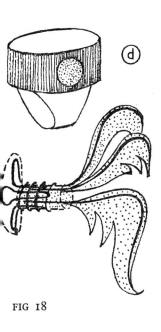

FIG 18

stretched over the shape. The form of the padding may be varied but it should always be firmly fixed to a cummerbund or to a calico foundation of some kind, so that it does not move out of place. The garment itself could be made out of wool jersey, cotton stockinette (cotton jersey), calico or hessian according to the kind of animal which is being represented and it can be sprayed and painted to fit in with the style of the head-dress. An example of this method is shown in the drawing of the elephant costume fig. 17 (a). The papier-mâché head-dress is built on to a skull cap and has a trunk which could be made of coiled wire like a spring, over which a tube of material is fitted. The wire can be coiled round a cardboard tube of suitable diameter and when the required length has been reached the tube may be slipped away. Be sure that the end of the wire is protected in some way otherwise it can be rather dangerous. The same material which covers the trunk may also be applied to the mask or the mask may be painted in such a way that the two blend together satisfactorily.

The two-man animal is most commonly encountered in pantomimes, but there is no reason why it should be limited to this sphere; it could be used for any four-legged beast which is comic in character. Fig. 17 (e) explains the principle of the costume. The two men each need a pair of trousers identical in colour and material with that used for the third part of the costume which is the body, and which links the two actors together. This is attached to the animal's head, which is worn by the front man. This communal part of the outfit needs to be capacious, so that there is plenty of room for movement and for any particular actions which are included in the script. The design of the costume should exaggerate the comic aspect of the animal and very often a toy-like quality will be found to be appropriate. The mane can be made from lengths of string bound together to make tassels and stitched on to a length of carpet braid (f) or a strip of material, which can be inserted into the seam which runs down the back of the horse's neck.

The lion which is shown in the same illustration has a costume based on a leotard. The papier-mâché face mask is attached to a fabric hood fig. 17 (h), on to this lumps of tow (or fine raffia) are either stuck or stitched and some stiff broom bristles are used for whiskers (g). Tow can also be added to felt mittens to make the paws.

The trickiest aspect of costumes for animals and birds is the fixing of tails and wings so that they are quite rigid and have no tendency to droop. In the case of tails it usually means that they should be attached very firmly to some sort of belt or jock-strap. The tail itself may be made of sturdy rope or a tube of material stuffed with either foam rubber or kapok and supported, where it is attached to the body by a wire foundation. This holds the base of the tail away from the bottom of the back and prevents it from hanging limply. The wires should be stitched into the tail and the loops attached to a disc of thick leather or industrial felt. Fig. 18 will explain this. Fig. 18 (a) shows a wire support; the join in the wire may be bound with finer wire or soldered and three or four of these supports will be required (b). (c) shows the method of attaching the tail to the leather disc. Holes should be pierced in the disc with an awl and then a darning needle should be threaded with carpet thread and the needle passed through the holes to secure the wire loops to the leather disc. When the tail is fixed to the disc, this in turn must be attached to the jock-strap or belt. Fig. 18 (d) shows a method of making a cockerel's tail. Felt shapes should first be cut out and wired, leaving three to four inches of wire protruding—alternatively crêpe paper feathers could be used, or wired ostrich feathers. Cut a four-inch length of broomstick and bind the wire prongs to this. The broomstick can be fixed to the leather disc with the wire supports as previously described. The broomstick and wires should be bound with material to match the tail feathers, then attached to the jock strap, or elasticated swimming trunks.

The costume itself must be designed in such a way that a hole can be left in the back to accommodate the tail. If the tail is rather large and cannot be threaded through a hole, as in the case of the cockerel, then the costume should be planned so that it opens with hook-and-eye fastenings all the way down the back and these can be fastened above and below the tail.

Fluffy looking tails can be made from net gathered up in lengths like narrow frills and twisted very closely round a core of wires. A variation of tones of net looks better than the same colour used throughout. For construction of this tail, refer to fig. 19 (*e*). First bind the three or four wires with strips of net so that there is some purchase for the needle and then stitch the frills to it as they are wound round— the tail can be clipped to shape after it is completed. Tails made by this method are excellent for cats and squirrels. It is important to watch that the silhouette is good whatever method of construction or materials are being used and it is essential to guard against the tail becoming too heavy.

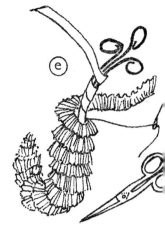

Wings present a very similar problem and almost always must be fixed to some form of braces and not merely stitched to the back of the costume. Wings for moths, butterflies and dragon flies can be made of net or gauze or some other very flimsy fabric stretched over a wire frame to which it may be either stitched or glued with some adhesive like Bostik (or Sobo). At the base of the wings the wires should be bent in such a way that they form a good shape which can be securely attached to firm elastic braces. The shape of the base and of the braces depends on the shape of the costume, as they will need to be concealed beneath it. The fig. 19 (*f*) and (*g*) give two possible solutions. (*f*) shows elastic braces and (*g*) the possibility of fastening the wings to a strapless bra. Fig. 19 (*h*) indicates one way of making a wire framework; the arrows *x* show the positions where double wires are bound together with a wire of a lighter gauge.

On to the basic construction, various decorative features may be added—glitter dust, sequins and beads to add sparkle—paint or a puff of gold from an aerosol spray. Feathers, small shapes of gilded leather, beads or even paper cut into small feather-like shapes can be used. Lightness is all important, both in appearance and in actual weight. Wings may also be made from lightweight acetate sheeting. In this case, there is no need to wire the edge of the wing but some wire veining will be essential and this must be extended to make a shape for attaching to the braces. Extra veining may be painted on to the acetate, and further decoration and glitter added to complete the design.

The designs for the bird costumes fig. 20 show an alternative way of dealing with wings. In this instance, the material forming the wings is attached to the arm and unfolds as the arm is raised and folds again when lowered. Made of soft transparent material, and decoratively sprayed and painted, they can be very effective especially for butterflies and moths; they are both easier to make and to wear than the more rigid wire ones. The bird costumes shown are very simple in construction. The first design fig. 20 (*a*) shows a straight tunic of calico or felt, with wing sleeves; the pattern for these being shown at (*b*); the dotted line shows the fold which lies along the top of the arm. Knee-length trousers are worn under the tunic. The whole may be painted or decorated with appliqué. The hat is extremely easily made and is constructed from the three pieces shown at (*c*). Add to these a beak, an eye and a bunch of feathers.

The second costume is based on either a bathing costume or a leotard and tights: over this is worn a half-circular cloak (*g*) to which slots are stitched. Through these the hands are passed. The cloak is fixed to the leotard at the back of the neck. A hood (*f*) is the basis for the head-dress, to which an owl's beak is added and an eye, which is built up of the three felt shapes shown at (*e*). Both the hood and the cape are decorated by dagging (crenellated or scalloped edge) (*h*) which may be cut from felt or some other firm material; contrasting knee-length socks are worn and a garter of dagging comes just below the knee.

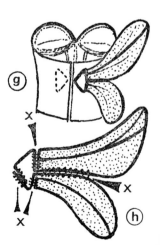

FIG 19

56

FIG 20

Fancy dress costumes

No one ever wishes to spend very much money on fancy dress costumes; the whole concept of dressing up is that it should be fun but ephemeral. Using everyday garments ingeniously by decorating them amusingly, or putting them together in a bizarre manner which suggests an air of frivolity or wittiness, is often one of the keynotes to success. Comfort should always be borne in mind—there is no pleasure in spending several hours at a fancy dress party in great or even moderate discomfort. Parties, even in fancy dress, are meant to be enjoyed; this should particularly be emphasized with regard to children's costumes.

Masks and disguises are always great fun, for they add to the air of mystery. A half mask or full face mask made by one of the quicker methods, or a cheap cardboard or buckram mask bought at a carnival novelty shop can be used and repainted or trimmed with lace or sequins. Cheap buckram animal masks are also available: they are very uninspired when left as they are, but if they are repainted and some extra decoration added, they can be made very amusing. Try wearing one of these masks with an all-enveloping cloak for a really dramatic effect. The cloak could be based on an old curtain or bedspread, plain coloured if possible, in which case it may be boldly decorated with painted or appliquéd shapes. A costume for a Hallow'een party could be successfully carried out this way.

A look around the house will bring to light all kinds of promising articles, such as decoratively patterned bath sheets, sheepskin rugs, even waste paper baskets and trays. Striped towels and blankets may be used to concoct the Mexican costume shown in fig. 21 (*a*). If towels are used two or more may be temporarily stitched together; bell-bottomed jeans *c* and a straw hat complete the outfit. Really old clothes will be useful for a tramp or a scarecrow (*d*). Use the odd touch of colour to add interest by wearing striped stockings *n* and scarf *j*, borrowed from the footballer of the family. Straw or raffia can be stuck inside a broken-down hat *e* and old boots

57

or canvas sneakers *i* are the best for footwear. Clown costumes can be built up from a T-shirt, a pair of pyjama trousers, a raffia wig, with an old bowler or top hat decorated with flags, striped stockings and hockey boots and white cotton gloves. A pirate is also a fairly easy character to produce: use a broadly striped shirt, trousers or jeans tucked into Wellington boots, a stout leather belt, a neckerchief, a head scarf, curtain rings for the ears, and an eye patch. Thinking along these kind of lines it is quite easy to concoct a variety of costumes which are inexpensive, and do not involve a great deal of work.

Most parents are many times confronted with the necessity of providing their child with a fancy dress for a school party. Sometimes this has to fit in with a particular scheme such as a nursery rhyme character, some hero from a children's book or a personage from some historical scene or geographical location.

As a basis, the child's everyday clothes will often help. Most children today own a pair of tights, a T-shirt, a pair of jeans and a bathing costume, and any of these articles could well provide a foundation on which to build. Four examples of the kind of costume which is very easy to achieve are illustrated here.

Firstly a design for Mary, Mary Quite Contrary fig. 22 showing a hat with a wide brim, preferably made of straw, which is liberally trimmed with tissue paper flowers and leaves (*a*). A frilled cotton pinafore (*c*) worn over a school blouse (*b*), the frill would look very charming if made from *broderie anglaise*. Coloured stockings or tights are worn with unblocked ballet shoes. The second costume is a design for Doctor Foster (who went to Gloster). The basic requirements are a navy blue school raincoat (*f*) and a pair of striped pyjama trousers, or old jeans painted with stripes, or a pair of striped or checked elasticated trews (close-fitting trews). Spats (*h*) can be made from canvas or felt and worn over ordinary walking shoes (*h*). A stiff collar is made from some thin white card and a spotted scarf tied at the neck (*d*). A top hat may either be borrowed or made from cardboard (*e*). If available, whiskers and crêpe hair would make an amusing touch.

For the Sweep (he could represent the character of Tom in *The Water Babies*) an old shirt, rather too large, is needed which can be torn and dirtied (*l*) and broken down jeans (*n*). A black stocking can be used to make a mask for the face, with holes cut for the eyes, nose and mouth (*k*). Over this a cloth cap is worn with wool or straw hair stuck inside (*i*). Black gloves (*m*) complete the outfit. Finally, a drawing of a milkmaid's costume (which could be used for the little girl in Jack and Jill) using a simple gingham or print summer dress as a basis (*q*). Over it is worn a white apron (*p*), for a hat an old-fashioned sunbonnet looks charming (*o*), but a straw hat with a daisy chain round it would do equally well. White stockings and black slippers will make the costume look very crisp and fresh.

Section 3

Pattern and decoration

Pattern plays an important part in the designing of costumes and it should be considered from the outset and not added as a mere afterthought. In certain productions it can be of major importance—especially for stylized plays, for ballets and for operas, when costumes are often designed around certain motifs. At other times, patterns may be used to emphasize character rather than for purely visual effect. The scale of pattern is always very important and this is something which is very difficult to teach; it is either an inborn sense or a skill which is slowly acquired by observation and patience. It is usually more likely that the inexperienced designer will make a pattern too small rather than too large. Border patterns become mean

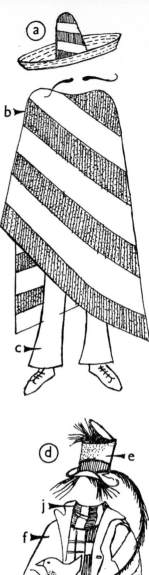

FIG 21

FIG 22

and niggly, motifs are drawn too thinly and tend to look apologetic; boldness on the other hand can easily deteriorate into clumsiness and vulgarity.

It is good to study patterns and not to simply make them up. The sources for research are practically endless and infinitely varied. Keep a notebook where there will always be a rich fund of reference to draw on. This should be made up of personal sketches of interesting and useful examples, as well as cuttings from papers and magazines and reference postcards collected from museums and art galleries. Do not despise the camera as a medium for collecting reference quickly, especially when travelling abroad.

Depending on the play in hand there is inspiration to be found on pottery and china, where there are frequently very elegant motifs. Primitive art from all over the world shows examples of very vigorous pattern work. For Greek plays the vases in the British Museum show enough designs for any number of productions. Plant forms and other natural forms should not be disregarded as these are the natural source of all pattern.

Always make a good-sized sketch before starting to work on the material. This clears the mind at the outset: no good result will ever come of work that has been insufficiently planned. It usually leads to a waste of both time and materials. Next, mark out the design very lightly, paying great attention to the placing and proportion, then begin work using the sketch as a guide.

There is a fairly large choice of ways in which to apply pattern; it can either be painted on the fabric; it can be stuck with various adhesives, or it can be stitched in place. Very often a combination of one or more of these methods is the most satisfactory way to carry out a design, for in this way an extra dimension is added. If the garment is going to be washed or cleaned, then a sticking process is not advisable. Otherwise, as a method of cleaning it is both quick and effective. Painting and stencilling with poster colours or designer's colours will not survive washing but can be quite suitable for costumes which are only to be used a few times. Painting with some form of oil colours does survive some washing and cleaning but even oil-bound gold paint comes off, leaving only a stain from the medium used. Stitched appliqué and embroidery will stand up to both washing and cleaning, but this of course is a much slower process. For most amateur productions, when costumes are only to be worn for a few performances the problem of cleaning may be disregarded. In the professional theatre, the costume is usually repainted after cleaning.

The paint can be applied in a number of ways, depending on the kind of pattern which is required.

If an all-over repeating pattern is required, it is usually best to use a stencil, at least for some part of the work. Stencil paper is a stiff oiled paper which does not absorb paint. Failing this, thin hard surfaced card (cardboard) could be used. But this does not stand up to as much wear and the stencil will have to be more frequently renewed. A one-inch lining fitch brush is better than a stencil brush for this kind of theatrical work and gives a satisfactory result. A stencil must be designed with regard to the ties which are the bands of paper that hold the pattern together. If it can be designed without them so much the better and to be really successful, the design needs to be bold and simple as any fiddly bits will soon tear away or the paint will dribble underneath. Separate stencils must be cut for different colours. The piece of material to be printed should be laid on a table on which several layers of newspaper have been laid out to give a sympathetic surface on which to work. Draw some guide-lines on the material with tailor's chalk to act as a guide when placing the stencil. It is not necessary to feel cramped by these guide-lines. A slight variation in the repeat can be very pleasing but the guides will help to prevent the repeat getting lost altogether or a distracting and unwanted slant from developing.

The thickness of the paint is important. If it is too thin, it will dribble under the stencil; if too thick, it is difficult to work with and will also stiffen the material, so that it no longer drapes or hangs agreeably. Emulsion or acrylic paint tends to have less malleability when dry than does fabric colour. With this latter a slight halo tends to spread around the design due to the bleeding of the medium, but this is not usually very noticeable. To thin emulsion paint, use emulsion glaze; to thin acrylic paint, use water; for fabric colour, use Brodie and Middleton's tapestry medium, or gold size and turps substitute (white spirit). Free brush work can be combined with stencilling very satisfactorily; it takes away from the rigidity of plain stencilling. If the pattern is being applied to stretchy fabric such as is used for tights and leotards, the garment must be worked on in its stretched condition, this means that it must either be put on a dressmaker's stand or be painted whilst being worn by a person. From time to time, the stencil must be wiped clean on the underside—always have plenty of cleaning rags handy. When working, see that corks are always replaced in bottles and that tops are screwed back on to tubes of paint. This not only conserves the contents, but also guards against the likelihood of spills and other accidents.

Painting will give a freer result than stencilling, but it needs to be carried out by a more skilled executant. Simple stencilling can always be handed to a careful, neat worker but painting can only be executed by a more experienced artist, who has confidence and the ability to draw. Fabric colours, designer's colours, emulsion and acrylic paints, or French enamel varnish may all be used, mixed to a convenient consistency with the appropriate medium, and applied with different-sized brushes. These brushes may be square-ended or pointed and both hog's bristles and sables will be useful. Hog's bristles are very useful for dry brush work and for stippling. Carefully position the work and sketch in some guide-lines no matter how freely the painting is to be carried out; this ensures that the right proportions are adhered to. Do not use too many colours in one design and do not make the painting so important that it is seen only for itself and not as an integral part of the costume. It is important to stand well back from the work from time to time so as to see it in its correct perspective. Also to look at it in conjunction with other costumes which are being made for the same production.

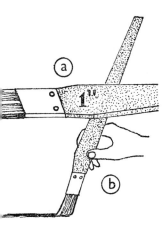

STRIPING of material can be carried out quite easily with the help of a yardstick or long straight-edge of some kind and a lining fitch fig. 23 (a). This is a brush which has an oblique-angled point and is commonly used by scenic artists. The straight-edge should be held at a slight angle to the work and the brush lightly dragged against it (b). The brush should not be over-loaded with paint or drips and blobs will be the result. For wider stripes, two lines the requisite distance apart should be drawn and then filled in afterwards. Checks and diamonds can be carried out similarly.

SPRAYING is a useful way of giving extra life to costumes. It adds a vibrance and interest to the fabric; it can also be used for breaking down clothes when it is necessary for them to look old and faded. Sometimes, when the pattern of a material is a little too bold, a little judicious work with the spray gun will help to subdue it. For very small amounts, a mouth spray may be used fig. 23 (c). Otherwise an aerosol with a power unit is useful. There is one on the market for which refills are available, which also has a detachable screw-top jar for the liquid (d). It is very easy to use, but it is essential that it should be kept clean. Otherwise, it will soon become clogged and useless. The paint used in these sprays needs to be rather thin and should be diluted with white spirit (mineral spirit). French enamel varnish diluted with methylated spirits (methyl alcohol) is very often better than paint. Another kind of spray to use on occasion is the aerosol, bought complete with paint. These may usually be purchased from a well-stocked ironmonger, they are especially useful for breaking down purposes. Silver and gold paint for spraying are much best bought this way, as the result is much more even. Coloured drawing inks are excellent and can be obtained from the manufacturer in large bottles. Although these drawing inks are not particularly cheap it will be found that a little will go quite a long way, also they are particularly easy to handle. Spraying should not be done in a closed atmosphere; see that there is an open window, or alternatively do the spraying in the open air.

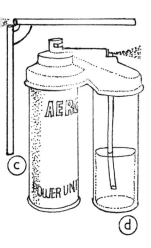

Release the valve by exerting very little pressure so that the paint or ink comes out evenly and not in uneven spurts; keep a fairly constant distance from the work, for general spraying keep the spray gently on the move. It would be advisable to do a little practise work before embarking on a job for the first time. It is nearly always better to do the spraying after the garment is made up.

A completed costume very often gains greatly from a little judicious spraying, it takes away the rawness from the work and gives it a richer tonal quality. To spray a group of costumes using the same colours from one to the other gives a great feeling of unity to the production and it is very often a good idea to spray them with a little of some of the colours which are being used on the set.

Extra textural quality can be achieved by spraying through such materials as coarse net or lace. The chosen fabric should be lightly laid on top of the material to be sprayed and the spray directed through net or lace. Spraying may also be combined with painting in doing pattern work. It can also give an added effect to rough dyeing and to tie-dyeing. Spraying is also quite practicable through a stencil but the stencil will need to be cut leaving a very wide border of stencil paper around it.

For all work with paints, mix and keep the colours in screw-topped pots or jars so that they will not dry up if the work has to be left for a few hours or even a few days; and always wash out all brushes after use. For fabric colours use turpentine or white spirit (mineral spirits), for F. E. V. (French Enamel Varnish) use methylated spirits (denatured alcohol), and for emulsion or acrylic paint cold water will clean the brushes, providing the brushes have not been allowed to dry. A final wash in hot soapy water is always good for the bristles. Plastic containers such as are used for cream and yoghurt are good for mixing paint in but guard against leaving these too long, as sometimes the bottoms dissolve leaving no bottom in the pot and a nasty mess to be cleaned up!

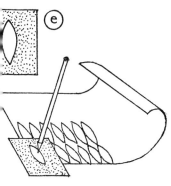

APPLIQUÉ is a fairly easy way of carrying out patterns, but it needs careful planning and it is usually best carried out in conjunction with some kind of painting and

FIG 23

FIG 24

spraying. For sticking fabrics a latex glue such as Copydex or Sobo cannot be improved on and for braids, beads, or for gluing to papier-mâché or canvas Bostik (or Elmer's glue) can be highly recommended. Various textures—thick, thin, rough, shiny—can all be used to give extra effect: make use of tinsel fabrics, P.V.C. (or any plastic fabric) and very thick felt. If a very large sack is made up from an old sheet and all unwanted scraps of material are stuffed into it, a good nucleus of bits and pieces will gradually be built up. Full use should be made of things like beads, string, buttons, thick lace, and both fabric and straw braids, for these can be particularly useful for building up chunky, primitive decoration. After sticking (gluing), they should be treated with paint, either sprayed or painted on, which will have the effect of unifying them with the background. Foam rubber being light and pliable, and being available in a variety of thicknesses can frequently be useful. It can be used either in strips for border patterns or cut into shapes and appliquéd in conjunction with other materials. Thick industrial felt can also be used in this way but any amount makes the garment very weighty. It is tough to work with and needs to be cut with a Stanley knife. In this way excellent decorations for breast-plates can be built up.

The design for appliqué patterns must first be drawn out full size on a piece of paper and then a tracing taken from this. The shapes can then be cut from this tracing. If a quantity of similar shapes will be needed trace the shape on to a piece of firm card and cut a template—like a stencil—fig. 23 e, and run a sharp soft pencil round this on to the chosen material moving the template about to get the maximum number of pieces out of the smallest amount of material fig. 23 (f).

Draw and cut out all the pieces before starting to stick and if large numbers of pieces are to be used they can be collected together in shallow box lids and placed in a position conveniently near to the work. This makes the actual sticking (gluing) process very much simpler and quicker, as less time is wasted sorting out the pieces. It will be advisable to draw some guide-lines on to the work just as has been described for other methods of applying pattern.

TRIMMINGS The use of trimmings is fairly obvious but only too often the effect is unfortunate, looking as though they are a mere afterthought, and having little to do with the original idea. Often these trimmings are ill-chosen, either too weighty or too light, or of unsuitable or unpleasant texture. Nothing spells death to a costume more quickly than the use of an ill-considered lampshade fringe, or one of those characterless furnishing braids, which have for so long been synonymous with the theatrical costumier's idea of historical costume. Braids by themselves are very rarely successful, needing the addition of a little paint either brushed or sprayed on.

The designer should become familiar with the various kinds of fringe and braid which are available on the market and if possible keep patterns of them catalogued in some way; an address book of stockists is also a great time saver.

It should be noted in passing that it is far cheaper to decorate costumes with paint and with the appliqué of inexpensive materials than by using many yards of fringe and braid. This, of course, is not necessarily the case when working professionally as the by no means negligible cost of labour in painting jobs has to be borne in mind.

A page of illustrations of patterns drawn from various sources is given in fig. 24 with some observations on the way that they could be adapted to the decoration of theatrical costumes. They are meant only as a suggestion and as a guide to the kind of sources which can be drawn upon for inspiration.

The first drawing fig. 24 (a) is from a painting in the Pars Museum, Shiraz, Persia. The pattern on the skirt could be carried out by painting freely with a brush, whereas the design on the jacket would be more satisfactory as a combination of striping and appliqué. The pattern on the priest's costume fig. 24 (b) should be either stencilled or appliquéd. Both (d) and (e) are suitable for stencilling, the first (d) is a tile pattern from the Tchar Bagh Mosque in Isphahan Persia, and (e) is a detail from a painting by Lorenzetti. Free painting would be the best method to use for

the primitive pattern from New Guinea (*c*). The glass painting from Damascus (*f*) is a subject for painting or appliqué, another design suitable for appliqué is the lion from a fifteenth-century Spanish dish (*g*). Fig. 24. (*h*) shows a pattern from an Attic red-figured jug, *circa* 490 B.C. which should be reproduced by a combination of painting and stencilling. Finally, a border pattern from a first millennium jug in the Teheran Museum for which a mixture of stencilling and lining should be used.

DYEING Sooner or later the costume designer will wish to use fabrics in colours not easily available in the shops and will thus come face to face with the problem of dyeing fabrics herself. One of the main difficulties is to find suitable facilities; this is because a large dye bath is required for all but the smallest articles or lengths of material, and because the material must be boiled, which entails the use of an electric or gas ring. Also somewhere for hanging the material to dry must be available.

Having found suitable premises, it is worth buying a good-sized zinc bath, for without it results are likely to be rather erratic. A sturdy stick for agitating the material and a pair of tongs for lifting it out of the bath will also be needed: a pair of rubber gloves will help to protect the hands. A helper should be co-opted if at all possible as it is a great help to have assistance when lifting heavy wet material out of the dye bath.

Be sure everything is to hand before starting. Do not try to economize over the amount of dye to be used; aniline dyes which need fixing and steaming are not easy to handle, so use a commercial variety such as Dylon (Rit, or Tintex) which is cheap and reliable; these can be bought at ironmongers or on the haberdashery counters of most large stores. They can be mixed together to obtain the required colour.

Fill the dye bath with water and set it to boil adding two tablespoonfuls of salt; meanwhile mix the dye powder with a little hot water in a cup. When the water in the dye bath is very hot, pour in the dye from the cup and stir it up very thoroughly. To ensure getting the right colour, tests should now be made with scraps of material until a satisfactory result is reached.

Soak the material to be dyed in a sink full of water and when it is thoroughly wet take it out of the sink and lower it into the dye bath; agitate it all the time with the stick. Allow to boil until the colour is strong enough, then lift it out of the bath and put it into the sink, rinse with plenty of cold water, squeeze but do not wring out, finally hang on a clothes-line to dry.

ROUGH DYEING Sometimes a varied effect is required; if so, do not soak the material before immersing in the dye and do not stir the material while it is in the bath. When it is ready, wring out the water instead of squeezing it. A second dyeing using the same procedure, but a different colour or tone, will give further variation to the cloth. Finally rinse in cold water.

TIE DYEING will give even more tonal variation. The contrast between lights and darks is much more marked. Tie twists of material with string very tightly either at equally spaced intervals or irregularly according to the required effect and steep in dye until the required colour has been reached. Further tyings and dyeings in other colours can be used with very interesting results.

SPECIAL EFFECTS Dyes can also be splashed on fabrics or applied broadly with a large brush. They can also be sprayed on. For small areas, a mouth spray may be found adequate but if any amount of spraying is to be attempted it is advisable to use some kind of pressure spray; an aerosol is available for which a power unit refill is obtainable. Dye can also be mixed with methylated spirits (methyl alcohol) for spraying and this is useful if a small quantity is required of a more intense colour as a more concentrated solution is obtained this way. It is not wise to treat large areas in this way as the colour tends to rub off. Dye mixed with methylated spirits (methyl alcohol) is an excellent medium to use for dyeing satin or any cloth-covered shoes.

There is considerable difference in the way that various materials take dye. It will be found that certain man-made fibres do not give a very satisfactory result, so if using a fabric of which there may be some doubts, be sure to make some tests

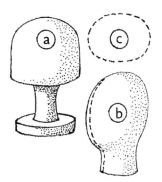

first. For very pale colours, cold-water dyes may be used, following the instructions on the packet. Helanca tights and leotards take dye very well, but need to be boiled. When dyeing woollen fabrics a little vinegar should be added to the dye bath.

Clear up immediately after each dyeing operation to prevent the dye powder speckling the next lot of material. Clean out the zinc bath and scrub the stick and the tongs so that the colour does not come off on anything else. Smaller articles such as gloves, tights, stockings, etc., can be dyed in a zinc bucket.

Hats and head-dresses

For making any kind of head-dress it is wise if possible, to obtain a head-block on which to work. If this is bought in a small size, it can always be padded with strips of felt or foam rubber to increase the circumference, whereas there is no way of varying the size of a large block. If many hats or head-dresses are likely to be under way at the same time, it is really necessary to have more than one head-block, for it is inadvisable to remove the work from the block before it is completely dry. It is likely to shrink during drying processes.

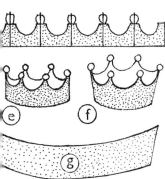

Two kinds of block are available: The first type, shown in fig. 25 (a) is made entirely of wood and the top section may be lifted off the base. The other kind, fig. 25 (b) is a padded block which is very useful when working with pins on materials which need draping and for working out shapes in straw or sparterie or even in paper. Recently a similarly shaped one in expanded polystyrene has become available. Note that the circumference of the head is oval and not round, as is shown by the section of the head-block (c).

As well as guarding against shrinkage and therefore finishing up with a head-dress which is too small to fit on the head, one of the other pitfalls is to build up a head-dress which is too heavy to be worn comfortably. It is surprising how glues and wire add to the weight and it is essential that the work should be tested from time to time to check that it is not becoming too weighty. It should also be ascertained that it is properly balanced and is not going to slip about on the head or to over-balance and that it is not too tall or too wide to go through arches or doorways. The question of weight is particularly important when designing for dancers or for anyone who is concerned with a lot of movement. It is always possible to reduce the size of a head-dress by sticking a small strip of foam rubber at the back of the hat. Paper patterns should first be made for height and shape as well as for size—see fig. 25 (d), (e), (f), (g). These show two simple crowns which can be made from card and buckram. Fig. 25 (d) and (e) show the shapes for a crown with upright sides, whereas Fig. 25 (g) shows the shape of the segment necessary for the construction of a crown with sloping sides, fig. 25 (f). The paper pattern should be tried on the head of the wearer before any further steps are taken for the proportion of the shape on the head and in conjunction with the costume with which it is to be worn, may not be fully satisfactory and there will probably have to be some adjustments.

Light-weight materials should be used whenever possible. Vilene (pellon) can be usefully employed for stiffening or net which has been sprayed with shellac. The brims of hats and the edges of head-dresses will stand up to much more wear and tear if they are wired with a light-weight millinery wire which can be either stitched, or glued in place with a contact adhesive such as Bostik (Elmer's glue or Sobo). Edges of crowns nearly always look better if they appear to have some thickness and for this piping cord (which can be bought in various thicknesses) or braid or even sturdy string can be used. These should be fixed in place before the sizing or shellacing of the article so that they will become an integral part of the work.

CROWNS (see fig. 26) Very simple crowns which are not likely to be used for a great length of time can be made from pliable card. If it is too thick, it has a tendency to crack rather than to bend. A wire glued in place around the base and wire spines glued behind each spike will control bending and thus give a variation of plane,

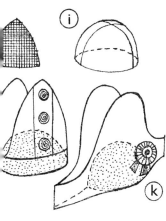

FIG 25

65

fig. 26 *h*. As mentioned above, a more pleasing appearance is obtained if the edge has thickness, and this can be achieved by sticking piping cord, a strip of thick felt, foam rubber, braid or string around the edge fig. 26 (*k*). For longer-lasting crowns buckram may be used, or strong felt, which, after it has been cut and stitched into shape, should be thoroughly soaked with shellac to give stiffness and to prevent the absorption of paint during the final painting process. The shellac should be applied with a two- or three-inch brush. It may be necessary to make two or three applications. When using thick felt, it is often better to use a knife fig. 26 (*s*) or razor blade in a holder than scissors. Not only is it easier this way but the resulting cut edge is much cleaner (*l*). Once the basic shape is satisfactory the decoration can be glued in place. This, of course, should be planned on paper first. Wooden domes, diamonds, buttons and other shapes can be bought cheaply from 'Do It Yourself' shops. These are ordinarily used for decorating home-made furniture, but are much better employed in building up patterns on costume accessories and stage properties fig. 26 (*m*). Shapes can be cut out of thick card (cardboard) or linoleum (this latter may be engraved with lino-cutting tools for further detail) fig. 26 (*n*). Cord, braid and string may all be twisted into shapes or interlaced to form patterns and then glued into place, fig. 26 (*o*). Beads, buttons, corks, small tin lids—all manner of oddments can, with a little ingenuity, be found both decorative and useful. These should first be fixed in position with a contact adhesive. When all the decoration is completed the crown should be given a coat of either size or shellac. When this is dry, paint the entire work with undercoating—a flat neutral colour is best. In the case of crowns which need to look gold or bronze when finished a coat of brownish or dull olive-green colour will probably be most satisfactory. On to this, metallic gold paint can be brushed, allowing the undercoat to show through here and there. This gives an extra three-dimensional quality and also avoids the tawdriness which a coat of flat metallic gold imparts. Glass jewels can be bought. These should be used with discretion and mounted in an outer shape made of cord fig. 26 (*p*). If they are

FIG 26

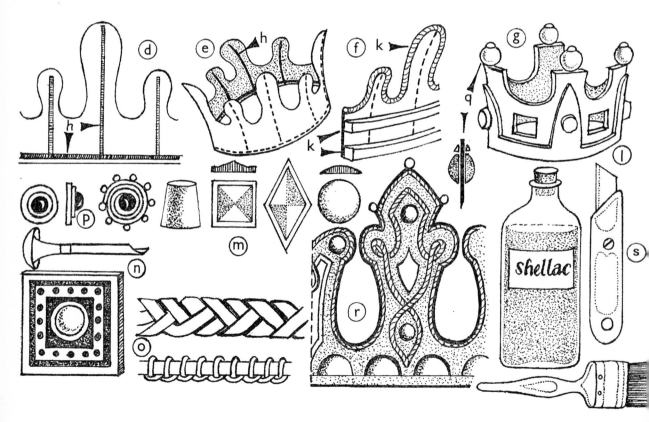

66

glued on in too great profusion or indiscriminately they add little to the richness of the appearance but tend to look cheap and amateurish.

These heavy crowns are suitable for characters in historical plays. For more fairy-like crowns or for coronets for dancers the head-dress needs to be light and airy in character (Fig. 27). It is advisable to work with the minimum of card (cardboard) or buckram and to build up the structure as far as possible with light but firm wire. If a gold or silver tubular braid can be found the wire can be pushed through the middle of this fig. 27 (*i*), *k* and *l* and then be bent into the required shape and fixed with a contact adhesive such as Bostik (Elmer's or Sobo) to a wired foundation made of buckram, card or braid, *j*. Otherwise the wires of the crown should be bound with tape before they are treated with shellac or size, after which process they can be painted, fig. 27 (*a*), *c*. Crystal beads or pearls, either singly or in strands, can be suspended from wire spokes which have been turned over at the ends to form loops (*b*). Failing crystals and pearls, tiny shapes can be cut from shiny gold or silver card, (cardboard) from P.V.C., or Beadec, or plain card (cardboard) covered with silver paper or painted with metallic paint. The main objective is to keep the crown looking very light and brittle. An alternative is to cut the shape of the crown from a fairly heavy gauge acetate sheeting, to wire the base and the spokes and then to paint this with a delicate tracery. A further way is to mount silver or gold lace, or pieces from silver or gold paper doyleys or cotton lace which has been painted, on the acetate with a contact adhesive. A sprinkling of tiny sequins (see the illustration for drawings of some of the shapes of sequins, bugle beads, and jewels which are available) will help to add sparkle. A delicate handling of materials is essential in this kind of work. A pair of tweezers (*b*) is a great help in placing sequins and tiny beads neatly on to a tiny blob of Bostik, Durofix (Elmer's glue or Sobo). For simple fairy crowns for school plays, crowns can be cut from foil-surfaced card and then decorated with glass and pearl beads or sequins fig. 27 (*e*). Fig. 27 (*f*) shows a garland in which leaves of net, felt, leather or buckram are cut out. A central wire vein

FIG 27

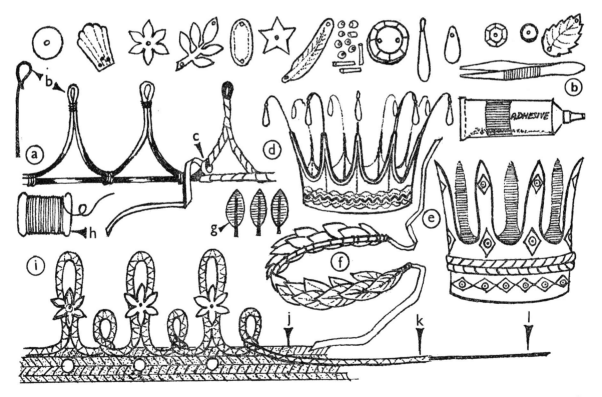

67

is glued in place on each. When dry, these are fixed on to a headband with fuse wire fig. 27, *h*.

HATS Some rather large hats and head-dresses are much more comfortable to wear if they are made in such a way that they can be fixed to a skull cap. The skull cap shown in fig. 25 is constructed from four segments of felt fig. 25 which are stitched together to form the shape (*i*). The segments must be adjusted to form the correct head size. After the pieces have been stitched together, a band of peter-sham ribbon (ribbed ribbon) sewn on the inside edge will prevent the felt from stretching. The cap can now be placed on the head-block. The hat shape should first be pinned to it and then after checking that the position and balance is correct this can either be stitched or glued firmly into place. For such hats as bicorns, or bishop's mitres or any very tall or wide hat or head-dress this will be found to be the most satisfactory way of making sure that the hat will sit securely on the head fig. 25 (*j*) and (*k*). The shapes used to build up the bicorn or the bishop's mitre could be cut from cardboard, from buckram or from felt according to what materials are available and for how long the hats are going to have to stand wear and tear.

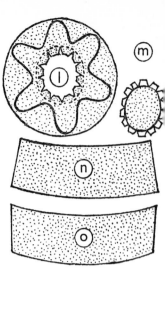

Tricorn hats of various sizes can be constructed from a circular brim wired at the edges and fixed to a skull cap, with the edges of the brim curled to form the three sides, fig. 28 (*u*), (*v*). Drawings (*l*), (*m*), (*n*), (*p*), (*r*), show the construction of Puritans' and Cavaliers' hats. Stove pipe hats, useful for some Victorian characters can be made as (*q*) and (*s*). Buckram hats are usually best when covered with material, painting is usually more successful when they are made from cardboard. To attach the brim to any hat it is neccessary to cut the hole for the head smaller than the circumference by about one inch all round and to notch it at regular intervals (*l*). The tabs can then be bent upwards and stuck to the inside of the cap part with adhesive (*p*). This should be done after the brim is wired. Very wide brims will need more than a mere wire round the edge, see (*l*), to provide extra support.

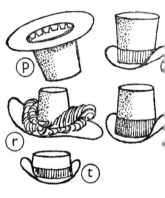

Straw may be bought by the yard in various widths, textures and colours, and can be stitched together by hand sewing or by machine to form various bonnet and hat shapes. Very cheap straw hats may be bought in stores, then altered, adapted and trimmed accordingly to fit in with the design. Also it is usually fairly easy to get hold of discarded summer straw hats which will make an excellent basis for theatrical work. Pale colours can be sprayed with French enamel varnish to alter them. If they have become limp, they can be revived with straw hat stiffener. Cleverly trimmed, an excellent result can be achieved. The trimmings need not necessarily be expensive if they are well selected. A certain amount of flair and style will make a hat or head-dress very successful even if the decoration is of coloured tissue paper, crêpe paper, imitation ostrich feathers and cheap ribbons. Charming flowers can be made from tissue paper fig. 33 (*i*), and from book (very stiff) muslin or net. Both paper and plastic doyleys can be used effectively and the silver or gold ones are often very useful. Dried leaves and grasses and seed pods can be used for decoration either used in their natural colours or sprayed lightly with paint, French enamel varnish or coloured inks. A visit to a zoo will often provide some feathers or they can be bought from a retailer. Light feathers can be dyed by immersion in not too hot dye. For stylized hats very decorative feathers can be made from crêpe paper and wire. The method for making these is illustrated in fig. 33.

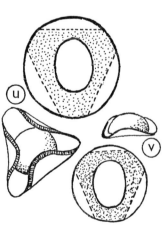

Very amusing and theatrical hats can be built up from cardboard and various kinds of paper. These look very successful in stylized productions, especially if the emphasis of the design is on the hat and it is worn simply with a leotard or some simple, uncluttered one-piece garment.

From theatrical suppliers and carnival novelty shops, it is possible to buy various kinds of buckram and papier-mâché hats fairly cheaply. Although these are not very satisfactory in their virgin form, they can often be painted, trimmed and doctored to create quite witty and attractive head-gear. If a large number of identically shaped hats is required buying existing shapes is a great time-saver and more time can be given to the decoration.

FIG 28

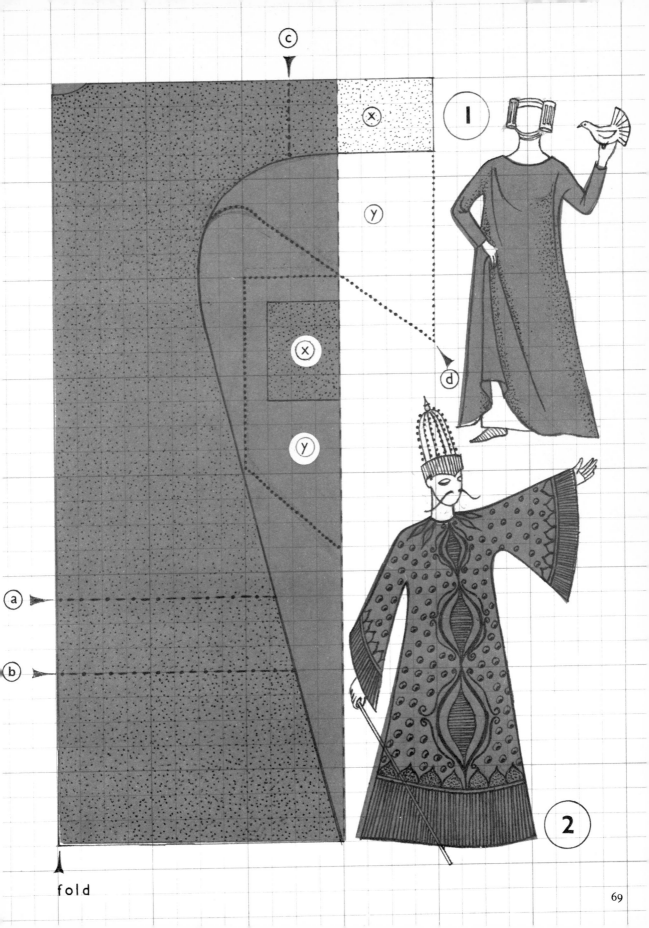

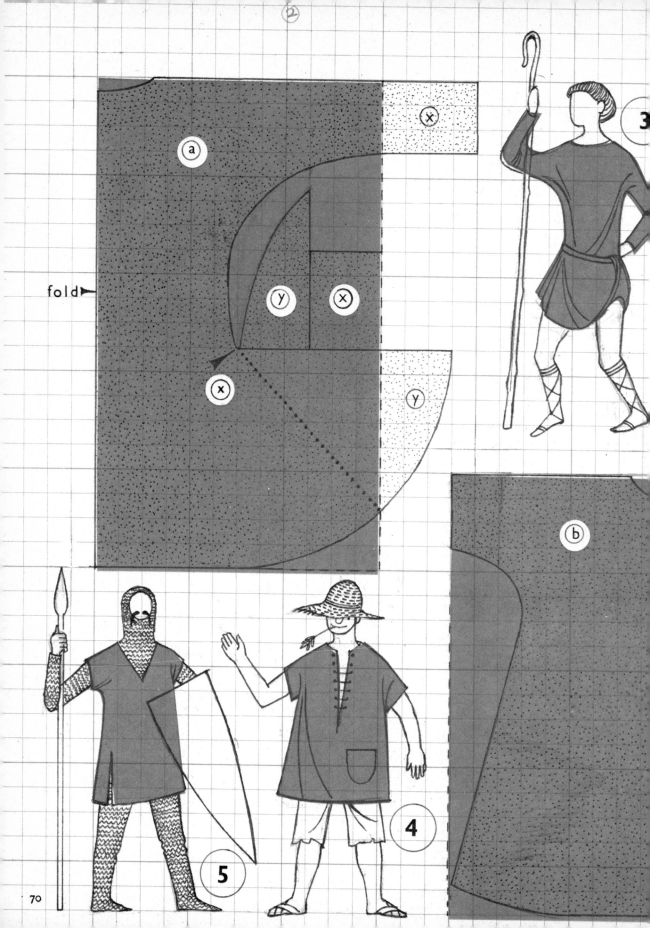

fold ▶

a

x

y x

x

y

b

3

4

5

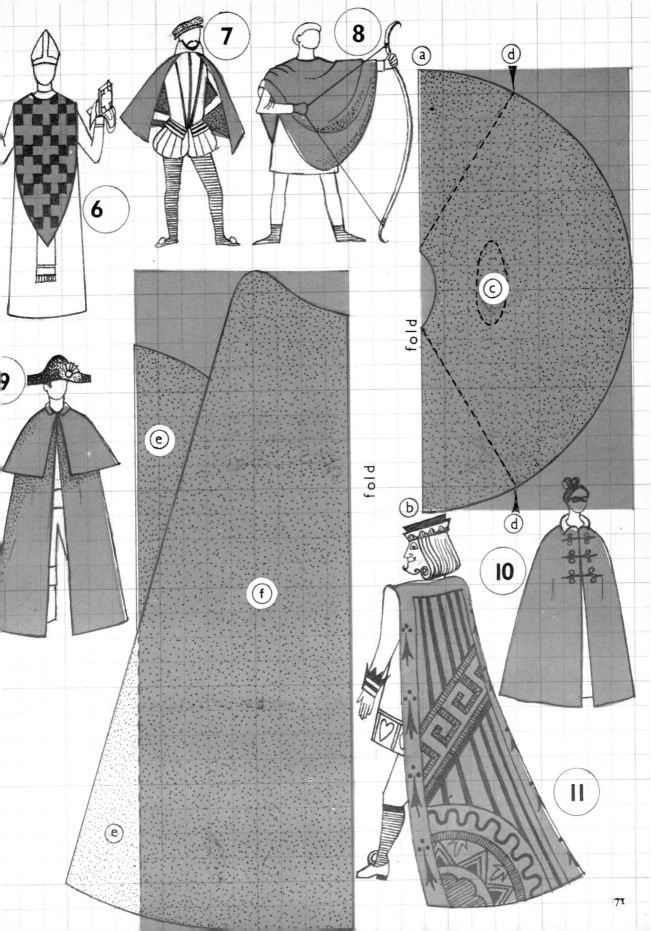

7

8

6

a

d

c

fold

9

e

fold

b

e

f

d

10

11

171

fold

© c   © c

© d

ⓐ a

ⓑ b

g   g

h   i

k   j

g   g

16

17

18

19

20

21

22

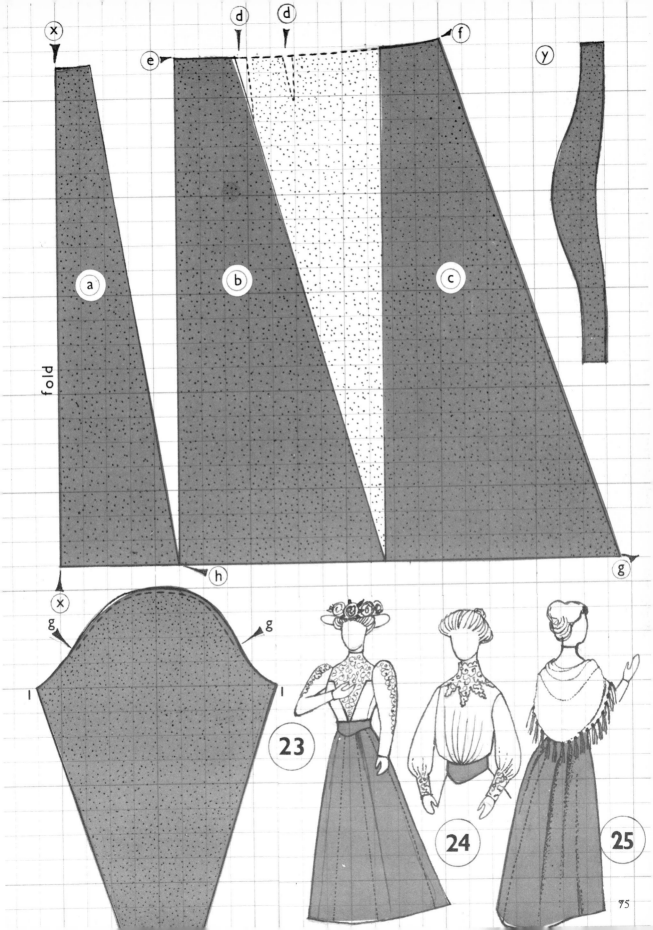

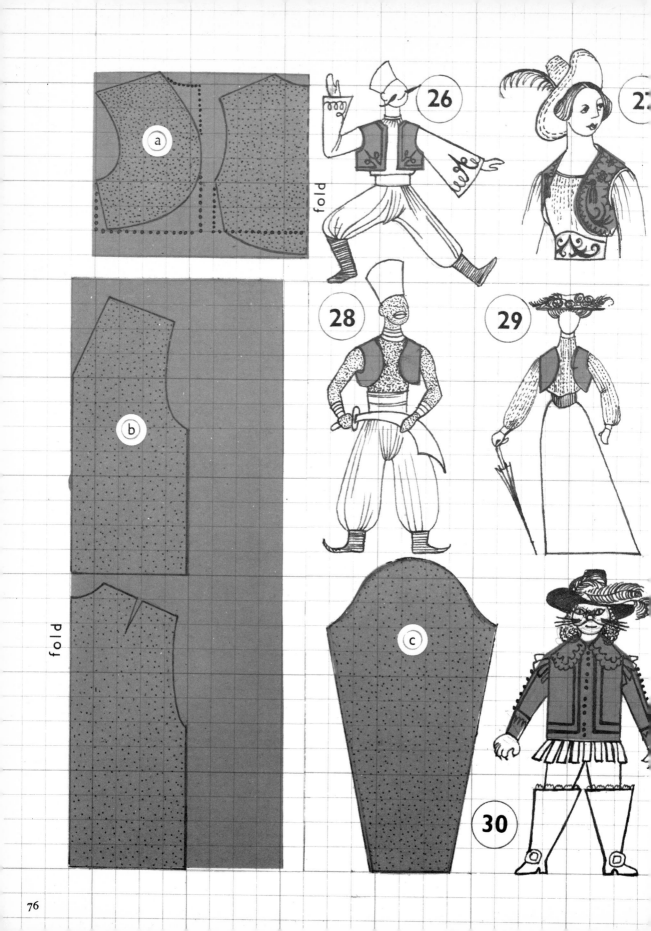

fold

fold

a

b

c

26

27

28

29

30

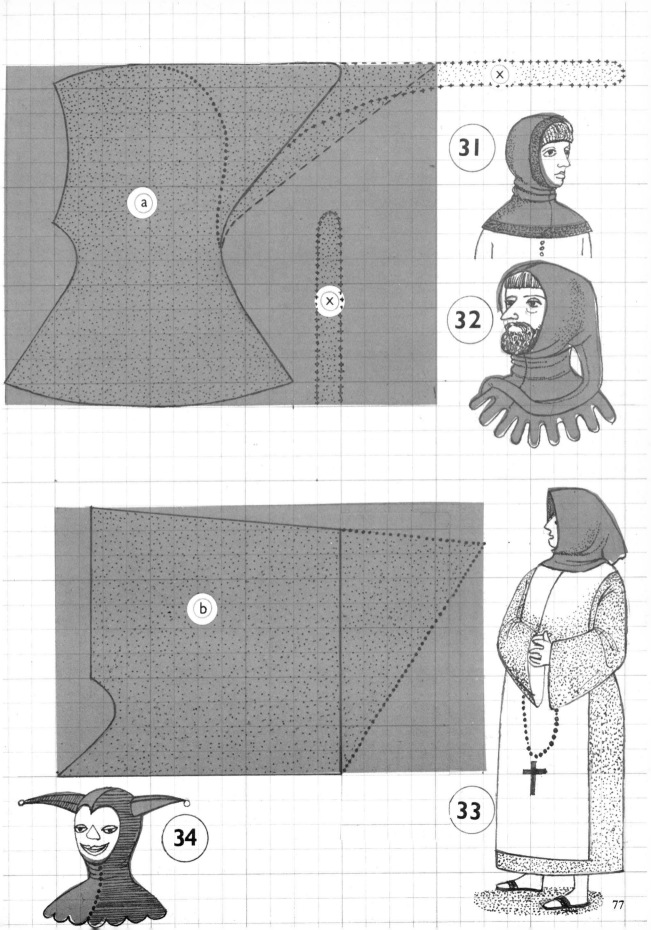

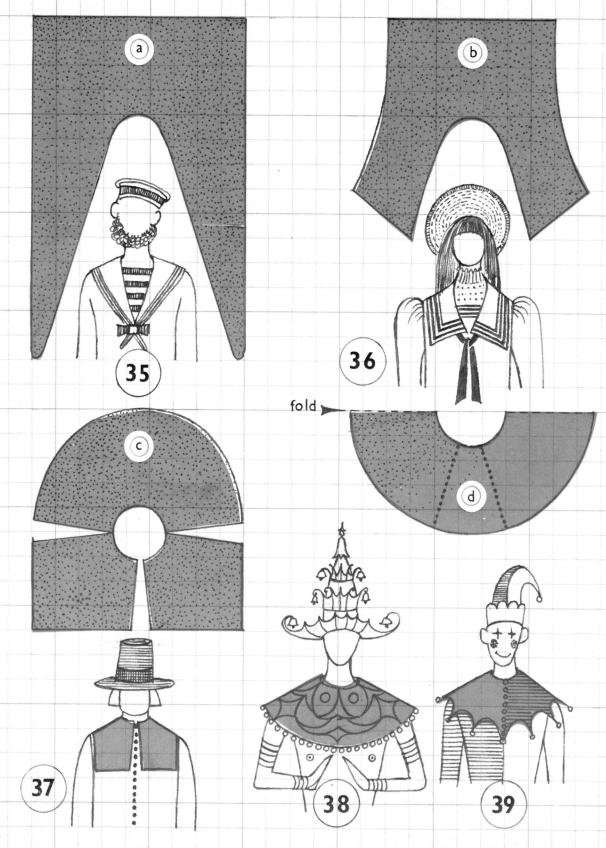

fold

The illustration fig. 29 shows a number of different kinds of hats. The first one fig. 29 (a) is a Maximillian hat from sixteenth-century Germany. It is particularly theatrical and could be made from felt or buckram or even card (cardboard) and trimmed with feathers. Ostrich feathers made from crêpe paper as described in fig. 33 would look very effective. Next fig. 29 (b), shows a straw hat, very simple in shape which could be worn as a garden hat or a summer hat for unsophisticated characters in the eighteenth or nineteenth centuries. The Edwardian lady's hat (c) would be best constructed on a straw foundation. The brim has been wired so that it may be bent into shape. The basic shape in this case has been trimmed with spotted net and a stuffed bird. Feathers, flowers, ribbons, cherries, decorative grasses and many other trimmings would be equally suitable. (d) shows an elaborate turban for a woman of the 1820s which would be worn to evening parties. Light-weight material should be draped over a very light stiff foundation. The hat foundations, which can be bought extremely cheaply on haberdashery counters or in sewing departments of big stores are ideal for this purpose. Otherwise a foundation should be made of net which can be stiffened with shellac. The fontange depicted in (g) is a net, lace or cambric cap with lappets and at the front a pleated lace fan which is wired so that it stands erect on the head. This was popular during the reign of William and Mary. Fig. 29 (e) is also a lace cap, trimmed with ribbon and worn in the eighteenth century. (f) is another cap of the same period, trimmed with pleating and tied under the chin.

The boater hat (h) is tied on to the head with veiling or fine net and is worn this way for motoring or for cycling, or at the seaside for holding the hat on the head in a stiff breeze! The Grecian head-dress (i) as well as making a support for the hair is very decorative. The shapes could be cut from buckram or felt which is treated with shellac to stiffen it and after a basic painting the decoration can be added. In this case appliqué would be the most suitable method of decoration, using small pieces cut from gold or bronze foil, beadec, leather or P.V.C. Some braid could also

FIG 29

FIG 30

be incorporated into the design. The Stuart woman's hat (*j*) can be constructed from stiffened felt or from buckram and it is trimmed with a cord and a small feather. The brim must be wired and then bent to make a becoming shape. Muslin, organdie or cheap tarlatan (cheesecloth) are used for the very charming late eighteenth-century and early nineteenth-century cap. The large size is to accommodate the elaborate coiffeur. It is worn both indoors and out (*k*). The modest mid-Victorian bonnet has a basic shape cut from buckram or sparterie and this has been covered with a ruched fabric and trimmed with roses. Very often the inside of the bonnet is ruched too; the Victorian bonnet of the middle of the century conceals the face except from the front (*l*). Finally, a straw cloche from the 1920s (*m*). These are of felt or straw; very often they may be picked up in second-hand shops, or people have them stowed away in trunks in their attics. They are surprisingly becoming.

Masks

Masks in papier-mâché can be made by the positive or negative method, depending on the number of masks required. Where only one mask is called for the positive method is quite satisfactory, but if two or more identical masks are needed, then they should be made by the negative method involving the use of a mould.

First make a drawing to work from, so that the idea is quite clearly established in the mind. Then take the basic measurements—chin to hair-line, face width, position of nose, etc., and draft them out on a modelling board fig. 30 (*b*). Then with a lump of clay or plasticine (*a*), model the mask on the board (*c*), watching that the contour is sufficiently rounded—a common failing is to make the mask too flat, so that it does not fit comfortably on to the face. Finish the clay smoothly. Now grease the surface with petroleum jelly, using a paint-brush if there are any intricate forms. Tear up a quantity of newspaper into small pieces. Mix some cold-water paste, such as Tapwata, and paste the newspaper pieces all over the clay shape until there are about six layers (*d*). Then leave in a warm place to dry.

When the paper has completely dried out, ease it gently away from the clay, using the fingers or a blunt knife (*e*). Paste another layer of paper on to the inside of the mask and when it is quite dry give it a coat of shellac to harden it. With a sharp blade (*i*) cut out spaces for eyes, nose and mouth, and trim the edge with scissors. Be sure that the mask is easy to see and to breathe through.

The mask is now ready for painting—either with poster, emulsion or acrylic paints. If poster paints are used, they will need to be varnished.

If more than one mask is wanted, then a plaster of Paris mould must be made from the positive clay model. This must have no undercutting, or it will be impossible to pull the mask out of the mould without tearing it. After modelling the clay on a board, a cardboard wall fig. 30 *l* must be built around it to prevent the plaster running away. Fix the cardboard in place with pieces of gum strip (gummed tape) *m*. The plaster must be applied in two operations. Always add the plaster to the water and not the other way round. Otherwise, it will become very lumpy and a weak mould will result. Put the requisite amount of water into a bowl. Then slowly sieve the powder into the water making sure that there are no lumps. Let a mound of plaster arise above the water before you start to mix with the left hand, whilst still slowly sifting in the plaster with the right hand. The work must be done fairly quickly as the mixture begins to thicken and set in a very short time. This operation is not difficult after some experience has been gained but the first time it may prove a little difficult. For the first coat, a thin and rather runny plaster should be used and this is dribbled all over the surface of the mask until it is completely coated and no gaps left. Next, a thicker plaster is mixed up (about the thickness of double cream) and with this the mask is coated thickly fig. 30 (*f*).

Leave the cast to set for a little while. Then peel away the cardboard wall and take out the clay. Use a brush to remove any particles which may be lodged in the

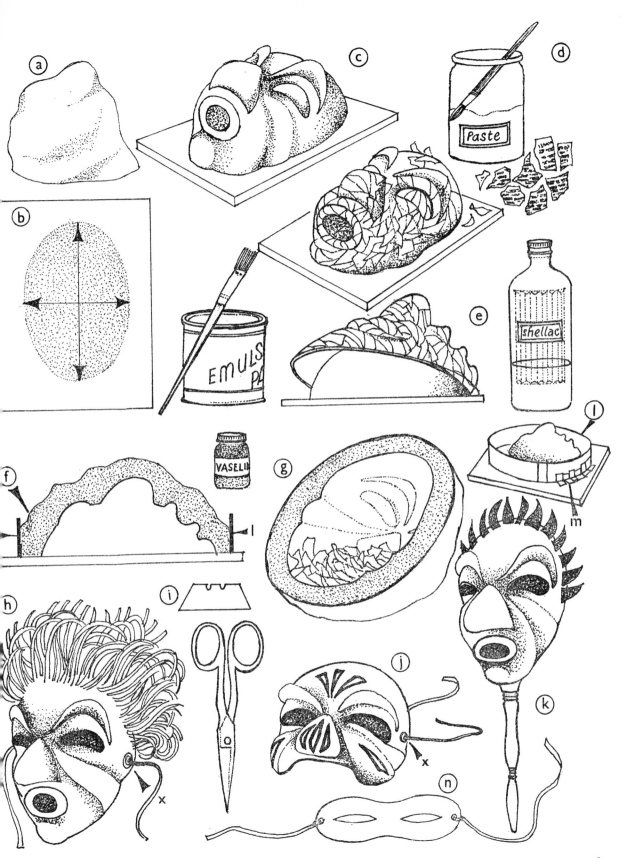

a

b

c

d

Paste

e

shellac

f

VASELIN

g

h

i

j

k

l

m

n

o

x

EMULS

FIG 31

corners. Allow to dry, then grease thoroughly with petroleum jelly, making sure that every crevice is penetrated. The mould is now lined with pasted, torn up newspaper in exactly the same way as in making the mask for the clay positive fig. 30 (g). It must be left in the mould until quite dry, after which it can be lifted out and another layer of paper pasted on to the greasy surface. When this is dry the mask should be gently sand-papered, after which it should be trimmed with scissors or a blade and then painted and varnished (h). Hair may be added and eyelets fixed at the sides x. Fig. 30 (j) shows the mask trimmed to a half mask and (k) shows a full-face mask attached to a stick with small fronds of leather or stiffened felt added for extra decoration.

Latex masks are very durable and if they are thin enough they are fairly comfortable to wear. In construction they are pliable in the mould; and it is thus possible to ease the mask away even if there is a certain amount of undercutting in the modelling.

Model the mask and take the mould in exactly the same way as for the papier-mâché mask but on no account should the mould be greased. Heat the mould in a slow oven until it is fairly hot. Then fill it with latex solution (the grade with the most filler) and leave in a warm place to set for about ten minutes. Experience will teach exactly how long, as this depends on the heat of the mould and the room temperature. Next pour the excess latex back into the tin. Leave the mould in a warm place until the latex is dry. Gently ease the mask out and trim the edges with sharp scissors; spaces for eyes, nose and mouth can be cut out quite easily. The mask should be painted with polymer acrylic colours, which may be bought in tubes or cans from any artist's colour-man (art supply store).

Any of these masks can have additions to them, such as pieces of felt or tow or feathers; these will be best stuck in place with a contact adhesive such as Bostik; or the mask can be attached to a cloth or felt hood which covers the whole head.

For domino masks, which are often very useful, it is helpful to have a mould of a face so that quantities of these may be taken at any time at short notice. They can be painted and trimmed in many ways, be covered with silk, satin or velvet and edged with lace or jewelled with beads and sequins. Wire antennae or stiff fronds of net may be added to the basic shape which is shown in fig. 30 (n).

The drawings of masks fig. 31 may help to give ideas and to show some fields for research. Notice in all cases the simplicity of form and the bold decorative quality which are characteristics to be aimed at. (a) and (e) show two differently shaped masks from the Commedia dell'Arte as shown on puppets in the Victoria and Albert Museum. (b) is a lion's head from Gordium which is in the Ankara Museum and which could well be adapted to make a mask. (c) shows a fifteenth-century devil, from the *Livre de la Vigne nostre Seigneur* in the Bodleian Library, Oxford. (d), a Commedia dell'Arte mask for Corviello from a seventeenth-century engraving. (f) is a dance mask from the Belgian Congo, (g), a wooden figure from the Nicobar Islands, (h), a sixteenth-century pendant mask from southern Nigeria and (i), a wooden devil dancer's mask from Ceylon. These last four examples are from the British Museum.

Jewelry and accessories

Costumes should never be overloaded with jewelry and accessories. A poorly designed costume will not be improved by decking it out with trinkets and ill-assorted pieces of finery. The jewelry and accessories should be very carefully thought out and planned as part of the costume from the outset. The scale of the pieces used, as well as the type of finish, are very important indeed; a cheap paste brooch will look ridiculous when added to a painted costume, just as a piece of very theatrically contrived jewelry made of gilded string would look completely out of place on a silk or satin gown.

Jewelry usually needs to be bold. When used in conjunction with very stylized costumes, plaited (braided) string or braid may be utilized ingeniously together with scraps of leather, pieces of card (cardboard), cork linoleum, bottle corks, felt, beads and other oddments.

It is a good idea to have a box into which any likely odds and ends can be kept, so that there is always a store ready to hand. Pieces of chain, old belts, broken necklaces, stray curtain rings, earrings and buttons as well as small pieces of ironmongery (hardware) may turn out to be exactly what is needed for the construction of a particular piece of jewelry.

Thick plaited string, sometimes using many strands at a time makes a good basis for belts. Leather, plastic and felt may be used in the same way but with different textural results. These may be enriched with wooden beads (which are available in various sizes and shapes) and also with curtain rings which may be threaded into the plaiting. Trouser hooks make stout and reliable fastenings. Fig. 32 (b2) shows a way of linking curtain rings g together with leather thonging f. This would make a mediaeval chain or belt. Dabs of contact adhesive should be made at each intersection. Another belt could be made from felt stiffened with shellac or leather if fig. 32 (z) is followed. This shape should be folded as indicated by the arrow and then a further shape linked through it as shown in (y). (a2) shows a belt made from engraved squares of linoleum c, which have been stuck on to webbing. Stiffened felt, or wide elastic d, wooden buttons add extra decoration e.

Fig. 32 (a), which is a pendant, is based on a linoleum foundation b, this has a raised cross added to it d cut from thick felt, or lino (linoleum) and is further decorated with twisted braid e and brass paper fasteners c. The whole thing should be given a coat of emulsion or acrylic paint and then gilded. Another pendant

FIG 32

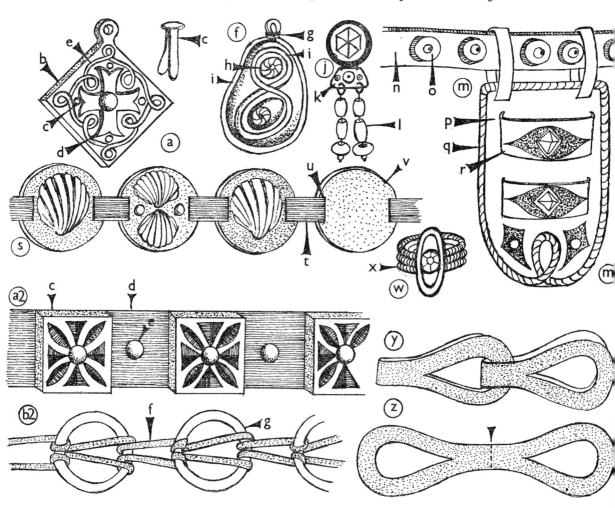

drawn at fig. 32 (*f*) is made from a smooth sea-washed pebble round which is glued some leather thonging *i* made into a loop at *g* with a twist of wire. On to the surface of this are glued beads or buttons *h* round which is wound more thonging *i*.

Fig. 32 (*j*) shows an earring; clips may be bought at negligible cost in the stores and on to these are glued decorative buttons or beads or sequins, singly or in clusters. A tiny shape *k* is cut from metal foil, thin card (cardboard) or acetate and suspended from the clip with fuse wire or cotton and from this more beads or sequins are strung. Fig. 32 (*m*) shows a sword belt with a hanger. The belt itself needs to be of sturdy leather or very strong webbing *n* which is decorated in some way. Here *o* shows a section of a cork on which a bead has been stuck. From this belt is slung a frog (sheath) into which the dagger or sword is slipped. This should be made of leather or felt (stiffened with shellac). The one depicted here has cord stitched round the edge serving the dual purpose of decorating and also strengthening (*q*). The leather strips *r* are pushed through slots cut in the leather (*p*) and stuck in place at the back of the frog (sheath). They must be strong to take the weight of the weapon. The hanger is decorated with appliquéd shapes and wooden beads.

Fig. 32 (*w*) shows a ring made from cord or string *x* which has been coiled around a greased stick and glued. Beads and buttons can be stuck to this with Bostik (Elmer's or Sobo) when it is dry.

Fig. 32 (*s*) shows another belt; discs of leather or felt *v* have slots cut in them *u*, through these is threaded braid or elastic *t*. Shells are used for decoration.

The construction of feathers from crêpe or tissue paper is extremely simple and effective. If crêpe paper is used, the grain of the paper should run across the feather.

FIG 33

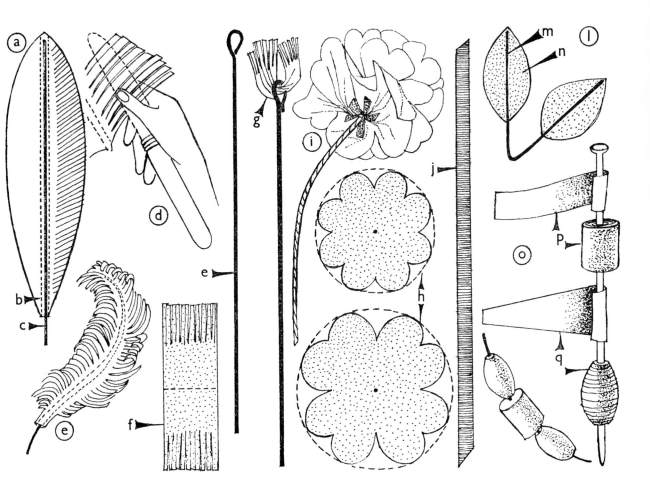

First, cut out the shape of the feather in a doubled sheet of paper and make two lines of machine stitching up the centre forming a channel into which a piece of wire can be inserted fig. 33 b. Into this slot insert a length of galvanized wire. Next, cut the fronds of the feather as shown in fig. 33 (a). After the whole feather has been cut take a dinner knife and draw the fronds across the back of the blade whilst the paper is held under slight tension by the thumb fig. 33 (d). Finally, bend the central wire into the required shape (e). For variegated colour spray lightly with ink or paint.

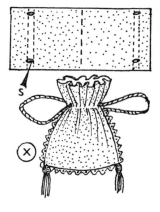

Flowers are best made from tissue paper as this gives a lighter and more delicate touch than the coarser texture of crêpe paper. First, take a length of wire fig. 33 e and bend it into a loop at the top. Cut a piece of paper and fringe the ends fig. 33 f. Thread this through the loop, bending it in the centre to form the stamens fig. 33 g. Next cut a number of petals of varying tones or colours as in fig. 33 h—about half a dozen of various sizes are needed. Smear a small dab of adhesive in the centre of each petal and thread on to the wire, pinching the centre to a depth of about half an inch. Automatically this will give the petals interesting pleats and frills. Cut a length of green paper for the stem j and bind round the stalk, starting at the bottom —a little glue on the wire will keep the binding in place. At the top, form three or four loops of paper to look like sepals. Fig. 33 l shows some leaves—these can be cut from paper or muslin for delicate results; or card (cardboard), felt or leather if something heavier is required. The shape of course may be varied, wire veins m are glued into position down the centre so that the leaves may be bent and twisted.

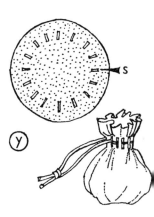

Fig. 33 (o) shows how very simply beads can be made from strips of newspaper. This is cut into long lengths, pasted with cold-water paste and wound round a greased knitting needle—p shows a straight sided bead and q a bulbous one.

Purses of various kinds are very frequently called for, because the action of the play calls for the stowing away of money or the giving of alms. A little research into contemporary sources will bring to light the kind of bag which is typical at various periods. A few examples are given here which are easily constructed. The reticule fig. 34 (x) is made from a rectangular piece of material folded in half, stitched at the sides, and with slots s to take a drawstring. This may be trimmed with lace, tassels or beads or in some other way suited to the period or character.

Fig. 34 (y) could well be made of a circle of leather or soft felt. Slots are cut into it s and through these is threaded a length of cord or thonging. Purses on belts were worn by men during the earlier historical periods. Two ways of fixing the purse to the belt are shown here. In (z1) the purse is cut in two pieces which are stitched together round the edge and slots are cut into the back s and through these the belt is passed. Fig. 34 (z2) shows a purse which has loops stitched to the back so that when the belt is threaded through these the purse hangs a little below the belt.

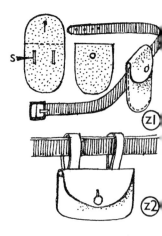

Ordinary fabric or leather gloves may be adapted to various periods by additions of one kind and another: fig. 35 (a) shows a lace frilled edging for a lady's glove; (b) shows the addition of a felt gauntlet for a man; (d) is a drawing of a long evening glove with a trimming of looped ribbon. Fig. 35 (c) shows a garter—these were worn by men in the sixteenth and seventeenth centuries. Two pieces of ribbon are machined together (at least twice the actual length needed), into this is inserted some wide elastic. The join is concealed with a rosette of ribbon.

It is not really practical to make fans. Unless old ones can be found (and they are usually very fragile), it is better to buy inexpensive Japanese ones and to paint them. In an emergency, very simple fans can be made as in fig. 35 (e). A length of paper is folded into narrow pleats, bent in half, and the inside of the fold pressed together with an adhesive. A narrow lace edging could be added.

Umbrellas may be decorated to make Victorian and Edwardian parasols by stitching lace round the edge. If spots or other shapes are cut from a contact fabric such as Fablon or a contact film such as Letracolour they can be peeled off again when the production is over without damaging the umbrella.

FIG 34

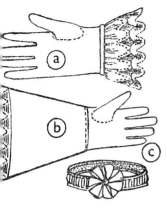

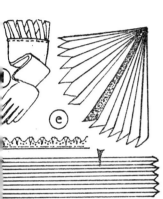

Footwear

Shoes being rather expensive items, a certain amount of invention must usually be applied to the creation of footwear. This often involves the adaption of already existing shoes and the conversion of them into an acceptable form. It is important that they should become an integral part of the design of the costume.

Quite frequently, an ordinary everyday sandal is suitable without alteration for use in Greek plays, or in mediaeval or biblical plays for actors taking the parts of disciples. Otherwise, a simple sandal can be made from a sole cut from stout industrial felt to which loops of tape are stitched and thonging threaded through these and laced in a variety of ways around the leg. It is sometimes possible to buy rope soles, and these make an ideal basis for sandals. An awl can be used to make holes through which the thonging can be tied fig. 36 (a). Shoes such as these will stand up to several seasons of wear for miracle plays or pageants should they be annual affairs, or should there be occasional revivals. An alternative idea which looks well with Greek costumes may be based on an elastic ankle support, usually obtainable from a chemist shop (drug store). These can be painted with appropriate patterns and the result is very effective fig. 36 (c). Boot shapes can also be painted on to tights or stockings which are worn with suitable sandals or shoes. The design is in this way extended up the leg (b) and (c). As in painting of all stretchy materials, this must be done with the sock or tight on the foot. It is usually unsatisfactory to do much stitching on to any type of hosiery material if it is fine in texture, because of the danger of laddering (running). If a row of buttons is to be sewn on to a thick sock to simulate a boot each button should be stitched on separately, not with a joined thread which will snap when the sock is stretched. Black ankle socks worn with black ballet flats will make quite pretty Victorian footwear and may also be used to look like skating boots. Spats made from felt, or canvas or leather are also very useful. These can be fixed with hooks and eyes or press fasteners, the buttons and buttonholes being merely imitation ones. Elastic under the feet will help to keep the spats securely in position fig. 36 (f).

A very easy way with mediaeval shoes is to use a man's thick sock and to wear this over a plimsoll (sneakers), rolling the leg part neatly around the ankle. When used this way, socks should be several sizes larger than the shoes. Otherwise, they are difficult to put on and if stretched too tightly they will wear into holes very quickly. In the case of designing for pageants, it is well to insist that performers should provide themselves with socks or footwear of neutral colours, to avoid the possibility of brightly coloured feet breaking up the unity of the scenes fig. 36 (g).

The addition of buckles can be made to stout walking shoes, plimsolls or ballet flats, so can rosettes and flat bows, and if necessary a large tongue may be built up which will change the character of the shoe. Old buckles can sometimes be bought in markets or in junk shops or carefully chosen belt buckles are usable, or they can be cut from thin card or celluloid and covered with foil paper (h), (i), (j).

Baseball boots, when given a coat of dye or emulsion paint reducing them to one colour will make quite an acceptable man's walking boot and of course the now commonly worn elastic-sided boot is perfectly acceptable as a substitute for a man's Victorian boot.

It is important when considering shoes, to give full attention to the height of the heel to be worn. One of the most unpleasant sights is the wearing of high-heeled shoes with a costume which should be seen with a flat heel or vice versa. This is a point which must often be discussed with the wearer, so that his or her co-operation is gained.

The addition of a cuff or false top to Wellington boots or to modern walking boots can be done with felt P.V.C. or one of the thicker types of plastic now available by the yard in most large stores. By varying the shape of the cuff it is possible to make the boot look suitable for wearing with a cavalier's costume or that of a Regency buck, or even a cowboy fig. 36 (e). It is possible to cut a canvas shape which

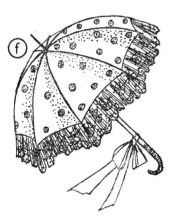

FIG 35

FIG 36

can be glued with Bostik (Sobo or Elmer's), to a plimsoll (sneaker), thus converting it into a hessian boot; this is excellent for certain types of peasant characters and can also be adapted for use in Russian plays.

Using a sandshoe or a cut away plimsoll (sneaker) as a base, by padding the toe of the shoe on the outside with wadding and covering this with material which can be either stitched or glued into position, it is possible to build up the shape of an Elizabethan bun-toed shoe (*k*).

Increasing numbers of men wear elastic-sided boots for everyday wear. These are perfect for use in Victorian plays. Those of reverse calf or suede look excellent for seventeenth-century shoes, with the addition of large bows of stiff ribbon or buckles. Leather and suede boots, which are in the wardrobe of many people can also be adapted. Fig. 37 (*l*) shows a boot trimmed with coloured Sellotape (any adhesive cellophane or celluloid tape) and flat buttons; fig. 37 (*m*) shows two boots, one decorated with Sellotape or braid and tassels, the other, with felt, diamonds and tassels. Finally, a short boot has a circular felt cuff trimmed with plastic lace edging (*n*).

Rubber solution such as Copydex is best used for sticking on to leather as it leaves no mark after the temporary decoration has been removed.

Section 4

The patterns

A section of very simple and basic patterns is included in this chapter. By using them singly or in conjunction with one another or by combining them with other garments quite a number of different costumes can be made up. These are not in any way meant to be a guide to historical cutting which is a wide and complicated subject not very well suited to the kind of productions with which schools, colleges and drama groups involve themselves. All these patterns are well within the amateur maker's capability. Before designing a costume or production it is well to take a little time looking at them, so that in designing clothes these do not become over-ambitious and beyond the scope of those who have to carry them out.

Very many variations on the patterns are possible: different lengths and necklines and shapes of sleeves can be used; different collars may be added and front openings will turn gowns into coats. By lengthening a bolero it can become a waistcoat and trousers may be cut baggy and wide or narrow and tight.

Together with the patterns are shown various ways in which they may be applied.

The scale used throughout is $\frac{1}{4}$ inch to 2 inches and all the drawings are worked out for well-proportioned people of average height. It is very simple to adapt them to the size of the wearer by taking the basic measurements of the person concerned and drafting the pattern accordingly on to sheets of paper or by drawing the shapes directly on to the material itself with tailor's chalk. It is necessary to have either a large table or a clear area of floor space on which to do this. The easiest way to work is to start from a line drawn through the centre back or the centre front and to work out all the measurements from this line. The measurements to take are the length from the nape of the neck to the waist and from the waist to the hem of the garment which is being cut. The circumference of the chest, the waist and the hips are always needed, as are the circumference of the base of the neck and the length of the shoulder seam. Other useful measurements to take include the distance from the centre-back to the armhole seam, from there to the elbow and then to the wrist taken when the elbow is bent. For trousers, it is necessary to know the length of the inside and outside leg seams. These are the absolute minimum. Other measurements should be taken according to the shape which is being cut. When drafting the pattern do not make it skin tight; an allowance must be made for ease of movement. When cutting out, remember to leave allowances for turnings. About $\frac{1}{2}$ inch is advisable for seams and considerably more for the hem. For inexperienced dress-makers, a book on simple sewing procedures will be a great help and will probably save a lot of time. It is useful to know the easiest way of dealing with facings, placket openings, setting in sleeves and attaching collars. Although they may seem very mundane and unglamorous aspects of theatrical costuming no garment comes into being without them! Careless cutting and shoddy making will ruin the appearance of any costume. If the designer fully understands the practicalities of costume making and designs with these in mind and the cutting and making is carried out with understanding and skill, then the completed costume will look exactly like the design as it appears on paper.

THE ROBE (Magyar) page 69 This is initially a mediaeval garment, but its possibilities of adaptation to other uses are many. It can be used for every kind of robe; for monks, for nuns, kings and magicians style 1. It is very similar to the robe worn in Arab countries today by both men and women. It can be full-length with long sleeves style 2, knee-length if cut off at the line (a), calf-length if cut off at the line (b), and short-sleeved if cut off at (c). (d) shows the line for a hanging sleeve. If the gown is being cut from 48-inch-wide material, such as Bolton sheeting, the extra pieces needed to obtain the sleeve length can be cut from the remaining material as

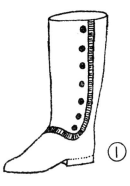

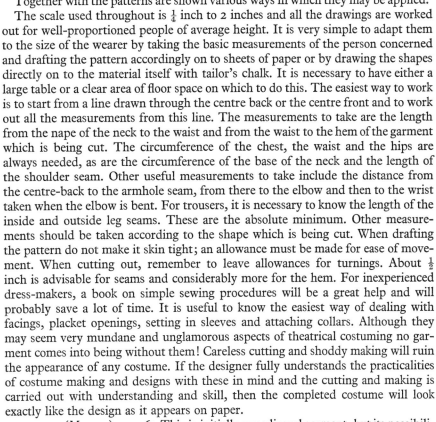

FIG 37

shown; style 2 (*x*) gives the extra material needed for the narrow sleeve and style 2 (*y*) the piece for the hanging sleeve.

DALMATICA AND TUNIC page 70 First the dalmatica style 3 (*a*) which is an early garment suitable for use in mediaeval dramas and biblical plays. The amount of swing in the skirt can be varied according to the shape which is required and there are a great many ways of looping up the skirt to make the garment look more interesting. Some of these are discussed in the chapter on miracle plays.

As with the robe, the pattern is laid out on 48-inch material. The piece (*x*) completes the sleeve length and the piece (*y*) shows the extra piece which will be needed for the skirt. The point (*z*) is the position from which to swing the arc for the skirt. This should coincide with the point of the hip bone. Quite frequently, a band of pattern or a contrasting band of material is found round the edge of the skirt. The second pattern (*b*) is the shape for a very simple tunic, which can serve a multitude of purposes. It can be worn by simple peasant characters of any period and most countries. With long sleeves it becomes a rough countryman's shirt and could be worn under a coarse hessian (burlap) waistcoat, or a sleeveless jacket of felt or leather. The one shown style 4, is a smock-like garment and has a centre front opening but it could be worn equally well without this, or could be opened from neck to hem. With shorter sleeves, a low neck and the lower part of the side seams left open as slits, it becomes a surcoat for wearing over string mail; the one in the illustration shows a V-neck but a boat-neck would be equally possible style 5.

THE CLOAK page 71 Circular cloaks may be made any length, but the most satisfactory one will usually be the one which reaches to the finger-tips when the arms are outstretched. The pattern is easily made by drawing a circle of the required diameter and then positioning the hole for the head. This can be placed centrally, as seen in the drawing of the mediaeval bowman in style 8 or it may be placed in such a way that the cloak hangs lower at the back than at the front, as shown by the dotted oval (*c*). For the cloak cut as half a circle the line (*a*)—(*b*) becomes a cut edge instead of a fold. This half-circular cloak is shown worn by the Elizabethan style 7. The dotted lines indicated by (*d*) make a cloak which is only a segment of a circle.

When worn by a bishop the circular cloak has become narrower on the shoulders. This garment is called a scapula style 6.

Two circles of different diameter attached together at the neck become a cape cloak (style 9). The Victorian lady in style 10 wears the simple circular cloak over a ball dress for a masked ball.

The second pattern (*f*) is for a cloak which is attached to the shoulders and hangs behind. It is worn for effect rather than for warmth. It is shown here laid out on 36-inch material. Quite often it is as well to line this cloak, especially if it is painted or embroidered as the paint and stitching show through on to the inner surface which is plainly visible when the wearer is seen from the front. It is shown here on the King of Hearts character (style 11).

Rectangular cloaks are not shown here, but they are extremely useful and present no cutting problems.

TROUSERS page 72 Two trouser patterns are shown, the first mediaeval (*b*). This is the same back and front and needs to be cut very amply. The real secret is to leave a long enough stretch between the legs. When made the trousers look a very unlikely shape and often call forth ribald comments from wearers but it will be found quite satisfactory. The legs are always worn with either thongs criss-crossed round the calves or with pieces of cord tied about them in two or three places, keeping the fullness in place as shown in the drawing of the shepherd style 15. If less fullness is needed around the waist without any reduction of the amount of material in the legs, the cutting line to follow is the broken one (*c*). Either elastic or tape should be run through the top of the trousers to pull them in to the waist and for baggy eastern trousers elastic may also be threaded through the ankles (style 12). For Russian breeches the bottoms of the legs may be gathered into a cuff which will slip inside the boot, the fullness falling over the top.

The second trouser pattern (*a*) resembles a pyjama and like the previous pattern, should be cut on the loose side. The broken line (*d*) shows the centre front of the garment and the line (*e*) is the centre back. Fuller cutting also makes this suitable for the Golliwog's costume (style 13). The clown's trousers (style 14) shows an example of an exaggeratedly wide cut with a strip of whalebone inserted in the top, to hold it away from the body. Whalebone could also be inserted round the bottoms of the legs.

ROBE, SLEEVELESS OR WITH SET IN SLEEVES page 73 This robe may be worn as a sleeveless garment or it may have sleeves which are set in separately instead of being cut in one piece with the rest of the garment. It is shown here in its basic shape by the cutting line (*a*). The extra fullness given by the cutting line (*b*) should be pulled into natural pleats at the centre back and front. These are kept in place by a firm belt worn rather high under the bosom. Made with sleeves, this gives a typical simple fifteenth-century countrywoman's dress, or would do well for such a character as the nurse in *Romeo and Juliet*, or one of the Merry Wives of Windsor (style 16). Cutting line (*c*) gives a sleeveless over-robe which could be worn over the magyar gown previously described in style 1. Opened at the front and using cutting line (*a*), it could be used as an over-robe either with or without sleeves. If the puffed sleeve for which (*e*) is the pattern is used, this makes a suitable garment for a wealthy citizen of Tudor times (style 18). To make up the sleeve, join up the seams *i–j* and *h–k* and run a gathering thread along the dotted lines *g–g* so that *h–i* fits the armhole and *k–j* the circumference of the upper arm.

ALL IN ONE GARMENT page 74 This garment is shown laid out on a piece of 36-inch material. It has side seams and seams at the centre front and back. A fastening must be made either at the centre front or back, a zip fastener being on the whole most satisfactory. The shape for the two front sections is shown by the dotted area (*a*). The two back sections by the dotted area plus the striped areas (*b*). The garment may be left sleeveless, or it may have inset or magyar sleeves (the latter being cut in with the rest of the pattern). Unless a stretchy material such as jersey is used, the garment should be cut amply to facilitate movement.

Some ways in which the pattern may be applied are suggested in the drawings. The clown's outfit (style 19) could be made of cheap cotton stockinette (cotton jersey) with the stripes painted on to the top half to look like a vest. For the teddy bear (style 20) fur fabric may be used. If this is too expensive, flannelette is a possible alternative.

An old blanket would make up well for the Eskimo (style 21), with pom-poms as a decoration on the front. Fur tacked round the edge of a hood makes the head-dress, and the boots are of felt. The last example style 22 shows an old-fashioned bathing costume made from cotton stockinette (cotton jersey) which has been sprayed in stripes.

GORED SKIRT PATTERN page 75 The pattern given here can be adapted to make two different kinds of skirts. First, the Edwardian skirts shown in the drawing of the lady wearing the blouse and hat (style 23). The skirt comprises five segments, in which the straight side is joined to the gored side, except at the centre back where two gored edges come together. This goring makes the skirt fall more pleasantly. Cut only one piece (*a*), with (*x*)–(*x*) on a fold to make the centre front panel. Cut two pieces of each (*b*) and (*c*). After joining the seams, stitch a petersham (ribbed ribbon) at the waist. The hemline of the skirt will have to be levelled. The placket opening is best made at the centre back.

The second skirt is a satisfactory shape for wearing over a bustle. Cut the front panel as for the first skirt. Instead of using four gores to complete it, cut two large sections, the shape to follow being made by joining up the corners (*e*), (*f*), (*g*), (*h*). Two darts are made as (*d*), (*d*) so that the skirt will fit snugly on the hips. The surplus material between the back darts (*d*) and the centre back is pleated so that it falls elegantly over the bustle (style 25). As before, the skirt should be put on a waist petersham (ribbed ribbon) and an opening left at the centre back.

Also given is a pattern for a shaped cummerbund (*y*) which will be improved if two or three little bones are stitched into it to keep it stiff. If worn with a blouse as in style 24, it will be helpful in keeping the waistline neat. The leg-of-mutton sleeve pattern is useful for blouses and bodices of the Edwardian era. A running thread should be gathered up between *g* and *g* until the distance *l–l* fits the armhole of the garment for which it is being made. The sleeve seam for this kind of garment should be about 2 to 3 inches in front of the underarm seam.

BOLERO AND SLIPOVER page 76 The bolero (*a*) is a very simple garment and the pattern here shows two variations. One variation has rounded and the other straight edges. The latter is depicted with a dotted line. Various braiding and embroidery can be employed by way of decoration. All kinds of material are suitable, but felt may be recommended for a quick result. Four different versions are shown in the styles 26, 27, 28, 29.

The second pattern is for a slipover garment which is recommended for various purposes throughout this book. It should not be cut too tightly and may be worn either with or without sleeves (*c*). Trimming and decoration may be carried out in a number of ways to simulate jerkins and jackets of different periods and styles, the use of braid being particularly helpful. It is shown here trimmed with buttons and braid and with ribbon loops around the hem as a suggestion for a possible costume for *Puss in Boots* (style 30).

HOODS page 77 These are very useful for mediaeval plays and are also used for monks of various orders. They can be worn by jesters, elves and other fairy-tale and nursery rhyme characters. The top pattern (*a*), shows different adaptations of the same basic shape. The one with the dotted line fits fairly closely to the head, as style 31. Of the three pointed versions given the one depicted by the line of little crosses is known as a liripipe style 32. The extra length needed for the liripipe can be cut from the surplus material as shown (*x*).

The second pattern (*b*) is a hood more suited to wearing with a monk's robe. It can be cut square at the back or it can be extended to a point as shown by the dotted line. Style 33 shows it worn with a monk's habit.

COLLARS page 78 Patterns are shown here for two sailor collars (*a*) and (*b*) and a puritan collar (*c*).

The circular collar (*d*) can be utilized in many ways: when fully circular it should be cut on a fold as shown in the diagram; for a collar a little less full remove a segment as shown by the dotted lines. Sometimes it will be found more satisfactory to shape the collar on the shoulders, to prevent a tendency for it to twist round in movement. The illustrations show how it may be used as part of a costume for a Burmese dancer (style 38), and also trimmed with bells as part of the jester's outfit style 33.

GREEK COSTUMES I page 79 Greek costumes are cut from simple rectangular shapes. For the woman's costume (style 40) the sides of the material are joined along the dotted lines, *s*. Fastenings are made on either side of the neck (*a*) and on the shoulders (*b*). The space *b–b* becomes the armhole. The dress is worn with a girdle over which the material is bloused.

The man's chiton (style 41) is made in the same way as the woman's but is cut off along the dotted line (*c*), so that it is knee-length.

GREEK COSTUMES 2 page 80 The pattern allows for an overfold. The sides are joined along the dotted lines *s*. The material is folded along the line (*b*) to make the over-fold and fastenings are indicated along this line. An opening for the head is left between (*a*) and (*a*) and the armholes are formed by (*b*)–(*c*). In style 42 the dress is shown girdled at the waist. In style 43, the overfold has been lengthened and the girdle tied over this.

The dotted line (*d*) indicates the cutting line for a knee-length man's garment.

List of Suppliers

BRITAIN

**Brodie and Middleton
Theatrical Artists Colourman**
79 Long Acre WC2
Paints, brushes, aerosols, stencil paper, glues, etc., tapestry medium bronze powders, glitter dust

Cornelissen
22 Great Queen Street WC2
Paints, inks, brushes, glues, etc.

Barnums
67 Hammersmith Road W14
Carnival masks and hats

B. Brown
32 Greville Street WC2
Felts and hessians

Davenport, Lewis and Co.
51 Great Russell Street WC2
Carnival masks, rubber masks, moustaches

Ells and Farrier
5 Princes Street W1
Beads

Frederick Freed
94 St Martin's Lane WC2
Tights and leotards

Fishers
Albany Street NW1
Theatrical cleaners

A. H. Isles
77 Gresham Street EC2
Bast and straw fabrics

Pontings
Kensington High Street W8
Cheap fabrics

Kettles
127 High Holborn WC1
Fancy papers and card

John Lewis
Oxford Street W1
Fabrics

Leff and Jason (incorporating Theatreland Ltd)
Soho Street W1
Cheap theatrical fabrics

McCulloch and Wallis
25 Dering Street W1
Haberdashery

Macadam
5 Lloyds Avenue EC3
Liquid latex

Romany, Ironmongers
52 Camden High Street NW1
Tools, glues, wooden beads, etc.

Russell and Chapple
23 Monmouth Street, WC2
Felt, canvas hessian, etc.

Walter Seiler Ltd
9 Stratford Place W1
Elastic fabrics

H. K. Small
Small House, 21 Foley Street W1
Pleating

Boots (any branch) **Woolworths** (any branch), **Winsor and Newtons**
51 Rathbone Place W1
Plaster of Paris. Many small articles. Artist's materials

Taylors
Brewer Street, W1
Buttons and button-covering service

USA

General artist's supplies
For artist's supplies (paints, inks, brushes, glues, aerosols, stencil paper, etc.), consult the yellow pages of your local telephone directory under *Artist's Materials and Supplies* for a store near you. Two large suppliers who will send you their catalogue and will fill mail order requests are: Arthur Brown & Brother, Incorporated, 2 West 46 St, NY, NY, and A I Friedman, 25 West 45 St, NY, NY

Craft Materials
Consult the yellow pages of your telephone directory under *Arts and Crafts Supplies* for a convenient store. American Handicrafts, 25 West 14 St, NY, NY, fills mail orders and has a catalogue of craft materials and supplies of all kinds

Millinery supplies
Most department stores carry a wide variety of millinery supplies. Also check your yellow pages for shops specializing exclusively in millinery supplies. In New York, the area along Avenue of the Americas, between 36th and 38th streets, is the center of millinery supplies, trims, braids, and miscellany. Don't overlook your local dime store as a source of masks and hats. Also consult the yellow pages under *Costumes, Masquerades and Theatrical* for specialty shops near you

Shoes, tights, leotards
Most ladies apparel shops sell tights and leotards. Also look in the yellow pages under *Dance Supplies*. Two large suppliers who offer catalogues and fill mail order requests are: Capezio, 1612 Broadway, NY, NY, and Herbet Dancewear Company, 1657 Broadway, NY, NY

Fabrics
Your local department store or sewing center will stock fabrics, braids, trims, buttons, etc. Consult the yellow pages for stores near you. Many New York shops specialize in theatrical fabrics and trimmings. Two large suppliers are: M H Lazarus Company 516 West 34 St, NY, NY, and C & F Fabrics, 1311 First Avenue, NY, NY. M & J Trim, 1008 Avenue of the Americas, NY, NY specializes in braids and trims

Theatrical cleaners
Any reliable dry cleaners will be able to do a creditable job of cleaning your costumes

Pleating and button-covering service
Raymond Miligi Pleating Company, 58 West 56 Street, NY, NY

Index